Sacred Death: Reclaim dying and embrace living

Overcoming our fear of death, dying and grief to enhance our lives and support each other

Catherine Shovlin

Section 1: Introduction…

About the author

Catherine has enjoyed a life experience spanning 90 countries and interactions with many talented and beautiful human beings. She is an astute observer, an End-of-Life doula and Shamanic-based energy healer, who has raised her 3 children mostly in London. She now lives with her partner sharing their life in Bali, Sydney and London. **Website:** Windsofdiscovery.com

By the same author and available on Amazon / Kindle:
Your True Colors *A practical guide to applying color psychology in your life*
Live Life in Full Color *A practical guide to balancing your chakras for optimal well-being*
Walking through Walls *Proactively challenging barriers in ourselves and society*

Dedication

I dedicate this book to my life partner, Lawrence, a constant source of loving support and unwavering belief in what I try to do.

Sacred Death: Reclaim dying and embrace living

**Overcoming our fear
of death, dying and grief
to enhance our lives
and support each other**

Catherine Shovlin

Section 1: Introduction…

Section 1: Introduction…

Table of Contents

Section 1: Introduction…

Section 1: Introduction

Foreword

"Death is under-rated!" was her surprising response.

I was proposing to run a workshop on death at her Centre and, as always, a little wary of the response. It turned out her NDE (near death experience) had created her unusual perspective, and she was a fan.

Hers was not a typical reaction and I'd like to address that. I have found that changing my perceptions around death and grief have given me more compassion, less fear and an enduring intention to experience life to the full.

So what's the problem?

Much more common responses in the face of death are fear, devastation, dismay, confusion, embarrassment – and avoidance.

Most of us have limited experience of death these days. We've certainly seen it happen in films and we may have experienced the death of a grandparent or friend or family member. But compared to the traditional village life experienced by our ancestors, or peoples in other cultures, death is largely hidden away in modern Western society.

And doesn't something hidden often feel scarier?

We may be hiding from death in our hearts and minds too. By not writing a will because it feels like tempting providence, by avoiding a bereaved friend because we can't think of anything to say, or by using terms like *fighting disease* and *cheating death*.

> *"Fear of death does more harm than death itself*
> *because it turns us into cowards, whereas death*
> *merely returns us to nature." (Robertson, 2019)*

Mortality is a big deal. Small wonder that we turn away from it. Choosing the invincibility of youth or to ignore that niggling pain that maybe we should get checked out.

Time for a change?

And yet, you have picked up this book.

Maybe death has intruded on your life and you're looking for clues. A friend has died by suicide, or unexpectedly from an accident or act of violence. Maybe your mother is talking to you about Assisted Dying or you have lost a parent. Maybe your best friend has been bereaved and you don't know what to say to her.

It could also be that you are curious. Maybe you are ready to come on this magical journey of death. Because it can be a precious journey. It can bring life into focus. It can clear away the detritus of good manners and unsaid feelings and lay us bare to our fundamental truths.

Or you may have experienced another kind of loss. The end of a career or business, losing your right to live in your own country, the end of a relationship, or the death of a pet. All losses trigger some of the same experiences as death, and offer the same opportunity to learn and grow, developing resilience and wisdom on our journey through life.

Deaths contain our truth about what matters to us. And who matters to us.

My hope is that in reading this book, you shift your relationship with death and loss. That you can reconsider your fears – moving them for now to a safe place, so you can retrieve them later if you wish to. And instead, just for now, for this journey with me, pick up your curiosity, an open heart, and an open mind. I hope that through this voyage you will find more peace, more comfort and maybe even touch the bliss and possibility that lie within our experience of death.

The 4 Gifts of working with Death

I have found many wonderful things about working with this profound moment in our life journey. Here are four that stand out – I consider them the gifts of death.

1. **Gratitude:** of course I am always grateful not to be the one dying or watching a loved one die. Seeing the value life holds in those last moments is a constant reminder of just how precious every day is – and how important it is to live it well. In a world where we are besieged with messages about what we lack in our life (and how to get it) then how beautiful to feel grateful instead for what we have.
2. **Compassion:** a deathbed scene will stir the hardest of hearts. This is our humanity laid bare.
The news cycle numbs us every day with tales of disaster all over the globe, so it is even more important to connect with our compassion – for ourselves firstly, to open our hearts, and then for others.
3. **Growth:** every death is different, just as every human is different. There is so much to learn, about ourselves and others, in every interaction. To learn not from an online training program but from real lived experience.

4. **Clarity:** we've all heard how nobody died saying they wished they worked harder. Expanding this message, the dying process is such a clarifying one. The things that don't matter fall away and the important ones – love and joy and connection stand bright.

You will find your own gifts too. Enjoy your journey,

Catherine Shovlin
Ubud, Bali, October 2023

First – hati hati on your journey

This is not a trivial journey that you have embarked on, and I urge you to treat yourself with respect, patience and compassion as you go through it. As they say here in Bali, *hati hati*. It means take care, but *hati* is also the word for the emotional heart centre. Be in your heart. Be in your emotions. Be true.

Before we start, I invite you to make the same shared commitments that I use in all my training sessions. We will be facing some deep truths, and this work can stir up long buried emotions and responses. Bearing these two commitments in mind can support the integrity of the process:

1. **Firstly, I honour myself** and all my experiences and reactions, past and present. I am not here to judge myself or punish myself for past behaviours, I am here to learn and grow. I will take this journey at the pace that is right for me; pausing for reflection or integration whenever I need to. I will be gentle and compassionate with myself and self-soothe in healthy ways when I feel the need.
2. **Secondly, I honour all others** who have been part of my journey so far. I will aim to avoid using my deepening understanding as a reason to judge others, holding them always with compassion and accepting that there is much I do not know that is behind their behaviour. I do not need to forgive any of them, but hope to understand them better, and learn from them.

I encourage you to reflect as you go, read this book in digestible sized chunks for you, and to use any of your regular self-care techniques to support yourself, and those with whom you interact. See later section on self-care for more on this.

Thank you for considering this journey. I hope you read on. Befriending death has changed my life for the better and that is my wish for you too. In the mud of fear and anger and grief there are jewels to be found. Let us journey together.

> *"Let death guide you into living a more loving and meaningful life"* (Ostaseski, *The Five Invitations*, 2017)
> *Frank Ostaseski, founding director of the Zen Hospice Project in San Francisco*

Gratitudes

I could never have made this journey on my own. I offer deep appreciation for all those who have helped me, in particular my teachers Hermione Elliot, inspirational founder of Living Well Dying Well, and Simon Buxton, skilful leader and guide of The Sacred Trust.

And so many others. Every client I have ever worked with has been my teacher, and every person who has come on my Sacred Death training courses in Bali or to Death Cafes I have run in England, Bali and Australia has brought their gifts and insights. I thank all the other End-of-Life doulas and palliative care workers I have had the pleasure to meet and learn from.

For opening my views on colonising and decolonising, I thank my daughter Imo, and teachers Kate Young, Sanne Breimer and Robin Lim.

A special thank you to the beautiful island of Bali, where this book was written. Her wisdom, her gentleness and the heartening abundance of my jungle-and-volcano view from my writing room could not fail to inspire me. The very different view of death and death ceremonies could not fail to inform my view. And the deeply felt philosophy of a people for whom community matters more than the individual and the ancestors are as real as those still living changes everything.

We are all in this together, all learning together. Let it flow.

Section 2: Our own death

My starting point

When I started my End-of-Life Doula training in 2017, I quickly realised I was a bit of a death denier. I was certainly interested in the work, it had called me in very definitively, yet in my heart I was still seeing death as something that Happens to Other People.

My brain knew this was ridiculous. Prophets and heroes, rock stars and great artists have all died. There was zero evidence to suggest I might be the one to "get away with it". I was kind of embarrassed to admit how I felt.

But it is not an uncommon sensation. Even if our brains do accept the inevitability of death, our hearts and souls may turn away from that truth.

Fear of the unknown is of course completely normal. And death remains the greatest unknown of our lives. Those with strong religious or spiritual beliefs may have faith and feel confidence that they are on their way to a hereafter, an afterlife. Research shows that having such a belief system helps at the time of death, bringing more peace to the process and a sense of purpose since in most religious systems a life on earth is seen as some kind of testing ground, or growing opportunity, which will determine the next stage for the ongoing nature (often referred to as a spirit or a soul) of that individual.

Such beliefs can also bring great fear at the time of death if the person feels they have fallen short or failed in this life and only judgment and retribution are waiting for them beyond death.

Section 2: Our own death…My starting point

Many who have had near-death experiences earlier in their lives have good reason to feel better informed and research suggests this greatly reduces their fear of death.

> "Results indicated that people who had an NDE had lower fear of death, higher self-esteem, greater mindfulness, and viewed death more as a transition rather than as absolute annihilation." (Journal of Humanistic Psychology, 2019)

But the truth of it is, however, strong your beliefs, none of us know for sure what is on the other side of the door.

Given our human tendency to live in the future (or the past – anything but the actual here and now) maybe that's just as well. Maybe life is meant to be about living, and only death is about dying. Maybe it would be a distraction to know for sure what's next or why we are here. Maybe it would shift our focus too much and detract from the rich possibilities of our lived experience – trials and tribulations and joys and all.

I was proposing to run a workshop on death and had tentatively approached the Centre's owner. A little wary, as always, of the response.

"Death is under-rated!" was her surprising response.

It turned out her NDE (near death experience) had created her unusual perspective, and she was a fan.

Hers was not a typical reaction and I'd like to address that. I have found that changing my perceptions around death and grief have given me more compassion, less fear and an enduring intention to experience life to the full.

Setting out on the journey

During my two years of End-of-Life Doula training - discovering so much about this great mystery, facing my own fears and sharing others' dying processes – I felt my view shift.

I was struck by how unhelpful the attitudes to death are that we can find in so-called civilised society. Working one to one with someone who is dying is sacred and important work, and I have the greatest respect for those who use the End-of-Life Doula training for that. For me, the bigger calling is to share my journey with others who are open to making their own journey to reclaim death for themselves or come to terms with deaths they have experienced.

Since then I have run my Sacred Death course several times for those preferring a deep dive into the subject. Through this work as well as holding Death Cafes and Grief Circles I have heard many touching stories. Dying is the crucible of the human experience, as sacred a moment as birth, and one deserving at least as much attention.

To reach out to a wider audience than I can in small group training, I have been encouraged to share some of that experience in this book.

Your journey

So how about you? Where are you currently on your journey with death? Understanding our own beliefs about death, daring to go there in our thinking, is an important first step on the journey. Once we can see clearly what we currently think, we can start to choose which of those beliefs and ideas we are happy with, and which might benefit from a rethink. It also puts us in a more transparent and self-aware place to have conversations with other people about death.

Let's look at some statements to start us off, and help you orientate your current position. This is not a fun quiz that will tell you which of the characters in Friends you are most like, rather these are some positions you might relate to – or not - to get you thinking. To self-reflect on your own ideas and assumptions about death. Some of which you might not have even noticed you are holding because, to you, they are as natural as the air you breathe.

For each statement I invite you to consider how much you relate to it. Is it not you - something you never fear or don't believe at all? Or maybe something you often think or feel? Or somewhere in between. Make a note for your own reference so you can reflect on what emerges for you from the process. It might also be interesting to look at these questions again after reading this book and see if you have shifted your position on any of them.

1. Your views on death

- I often think about my own death.
- I am afraid of death.
- I avoid thinking about death.

- If I knew I had a life-limiting condition, I would do whatever it takes to fight it.
- I often think about the meaning of life, of my life.
- I believe in life after death.
- I have spiritual beliefs which help me when I think about death.
- I hate to think it's all over when I die.
- I believe people have the right to end their own lives.

2. Death and Dying

- I have had close contact with other people's deaths.
- I get upset to see death and dying in TV/films.
- I often think about the fact that those close to me will die one day.
- I often think about those close to me that have already died.
- I am "good" at being ill, I'm an easy patient, I don't make a fuss or a lot of demands.
- I am "good" about other people being ill, I take excellent care of them, nothing is too much trouble.

3. Planning for death

- I have a legal document with my preferences for the end of my life (eg DNR, time on life support, preferred location)
- I have a power of attorney in place for my health decisions.
- I have a power of attorney in place for my financial decisions.
- I have planned my own funeral and shared my plans with others.

- I carry an organ donor card.
- I have made a will.

Considering all your answers, which of the following categories feel most like you? Of course you won't feel the same every day, but we all have a general tendency. Is it a surprise? Are there aspects to some of the questions that you would like to explore further, shift even?

Typical attitudes to death

Before we get into more depth, here is a brief outline of the main types of attitudes people have towards death:

- **Death Avoiding**: If this is you, you avoid anything to do with death. You don't want to think about it and change the subject if it comes up. That might help you avoid discomfort, but it can also mean a lack of realism eg not making a will, which can have repercussions for those around you when the inevitable finally happens.
- **Death Fearing**: Many will identify with this category. The very idea of death fills you with a sense of dread. You fear the loss of your independence and faculties as you approach death, you are worried about the pain that may be in store, and the journey through death – especially if your faith or own conscience includes a concept of judgment and punishment.
- **Death Denying**: You are ignoring the fact that you will die and may act like you will live forever. This can be a coping mechanism, but it may also mean you miss an opportunity for personal growth which could be found in facing your own mortality.

- **Death Defying**: You might be an individual with an urge to take great physical risks with your own life, taking up extreme sports or living recklessly. Or be someone who knows that they have serious life-threatening conditions which you will fight every step of the way. This may drive you to extreme measures to fight a life-threatening medical condition – eg travelling long distances for breakthrough scientific treatments or to see healers. This attitude may give you the energy and drive to prolong your life, or it may mean your energetic and financial resources are used up in the fight rather than facing other aspects of the death journey.
- **Death Loving**: You are fascinated by the subject and think about death a lot, it intrigues you. Sometimes known as thanatophilia, the fascination may be spiritual, anthropological, medical, artistic… whatever your drive, the topic is of deep interest and meaning for you and may draw you into death related occupations such as being a funeral director.
- **Death Accepting**: You are reconciled with and accept the idea of your own death, whenever and however it happens. You might even be looking forward to the transformational possibilities. You could be angry if you are resuscitated, and your family may not agree with your position. You are more likely to live in the present moment and cherish connections and experiences in the day to day.

You are unlikely to feel you are in a clear-cut single category. But having a sense of your general starting position in relation to death will help you identify which parts of this journey will be more challenging and more important for you. Though even if you are firmly in the first category, you have still picked up this book, so it looks like you might be ready for a shift.

It can be helpful too to have these distinctions in mind when talking to others. It is not our place to force anybody to change or to be in one category or another. This is a personal journey, and we always respect each other. Knowing where somebody stands can inform how we talk to them though and give us helpful clues about how we might support them. Asking them about where they stand on these statements about death is also an interesting way to fact-find and open up the subject.

I'd like to share some real-life examples with you of how these categories affect behaviour, to bring the idea to life. (Note that here, and throughout this book, I have changed the names to protect the confidentiality of individuals and their families)

Death Avoiding

This is the most common group. They wouldn't try to claim that death doesn't exist, but they don't want to be reminded of it. They avoid funerals whenever possible, even fictitious ones in films and deter others from talking about death – dismissing it as morbid or depressing.

In my experience this group are more likely to be those with no spiritual beliefs. They feel that:

"When you're gone, you're gone".

"You only live once"

"Life's too short to sit around waiting…"

Like any other position described above, this is a completely valid point of view. As an End-of-Life doula I would always work within my client's frame of reference. I'm not there with an agenda, peddling any point of view. And after all, what do I know? I only know what I think, feel, believe to be true. And that's a very individual thing,

It can be challenging though, to get a Death Avoider to make any preparations for their own death since they don't want to discuss it. One approach is to draw up an End-of-Life Plan (known in some countries as a Living Will) with them (see Section 7 for more on this, later in the book). If you really want to needle them into action, include a few things you know they won't like! Editing – or fixing - an existing plan that you have prepared for them can feel less daunting than starting from scratch, though every person is different, and some sensitivity is required.

I tried this approach with one client whose starting point was "Oh anything, I don't mind what happens".

Making unpopular assumptions on the subject galvanised them into action and generated this conversation:

> "Of course I don't want a deathbed choir! What a dreadful idea!"

> "Oh, I'm sorry. Any kind of music then?"

> "Classics of course, but not too heavy. And easy listening. Nothing rowdy or too modern."

> "Noted."

> "And what's this about pot plants??!! I can't stand pot plants. Get that out!"

> "Oops. My mistake. Cut flowers?"

> "I suppose. Just no bloody carnations."

The challenge for those in this group can be coming to terms with deaths when they do cross their path. Maybe they lose their life partner, or a dear friend. They are more likely to be stopped in their tracks by this event, having less experience of exploring their feelings on the subject. Supporting somebody in this situation once they are bereaved will take patience and some flexibility to approach the idea through different routes until you find one that works for them. And be prepared for what works one day to be no use at all the next. Grief is not a linear, logical process. As always, the watchword is compassion. Remember you're not there to take their grief away, or 'fix' them, you're just present for them. We will look at grief in more detail in Section 6.

Some of this can also be true for the Death Avoider when it comes to facing their own death. They may refuse to talk about it, avoid making any arrangements and insist on "carrying on as usual". This is a valid coping strategy too, so as with any other response we see in someone we are working with, we maintain compassionate presence, don't judge them for their views and hold space in whatever way works best for them.

It may be a situation where euphemisms or metaphors can help. You could ask them who they want to look after their dog if they have to go away. Or make gentle observations about other deaths or funerals so that their reaction might give you clues from about what would work for them.

Death Fearing

A young woman arrived at the taster day for my Sacred Death course. She looked pale and shaken as she took her place in the circle of twenty or so participants. As we progressed through the workshop, and especially during the group exercises she started to look like she was in serious trouble.

I took her to one side, and she explained that she had been raised in a particular faith where death was complex and unlikely to result in eternal happiness. She described herself as death-phobic and shared that she had had a panic attack earlier in the day just at the thought of having conversations about death.

And yet here she was. What an act of great courage and commitment to her own evolution. She was confronting her demons for sure. She ended up taking the six-week course and visibly grew in this area from one week to the next, leaving with a profound sense of comfort around the topic and the discovery that she had many skills that would make her well suited to working with the dying.

Death Denying

Anya has been told her cancer is terminal. There is an option to increase her remaining time from a few months to maybe twice that if she does surgery, chemotherapy and radiation treatment. As a lifelong naturopath she has never been a big believer in pharmaceutical medicine though and is reluctant to go through any of those procedures. She also has financial issues and is living in a country where she would have to pay for any medical treatment.

Most significantly, she feels sure she will get better, so she does not believe it is necessary for her to have any treatment.

Her close family have noticed her decline. She has good days and bad days but in general she is losing weight, getting weaker, and her pain level is increasing. She tends to suffer in silence, but they know the signs. Her posture is more and more protective of her body. Curling in on herself, her head bowed. She won't see a doctor about pain control though at a later stage concedes to the occasional over-the-counter painkiller.

Hope of a cure, a miracle, or spontaneous remission is common among Death Deniers. And can be useful. Hope can help the dying person adjust to the process they are in.

This stance can be uncomfortable though for close friends and family members, especially if they feel 'truth' is more important.

> "Why is she in denial? Can't she see what is happening" Jean's friend asked me.

> "Shouldn't someone tell her? She needs to face up to the truth and make some tough treatment choices! She's just going to die if she won't do anything."

Sometimes it is the family members who behave as Death Deniers as they struggle to adjust to the impending reality of their loved one's death.

> "It'll be fine. You'll be ok".

In these cases like this, it might fall to the dying person to help their family accept the truth – as well as doing their own work to come to terms with their impending death.

When I am confronted with Death Denial, whoever it comes from, I aim to treat it the same way as I treat any state of mind. With acceptance and compassionate presence. This is the person's truth. It might not be seen as rational by some, or realistic by others, but it is their truth. And very occasionally miracles do happen, so why not for them?

What I would also want to make sure of though, is that plans are in place so that if the expected course of action does ensue – that they decline further and then die – there is no need for a last-minute panic to manage end-of-life symptom control, medical needs, family visits or funeral arrangements.

It's never too early to make any of these plans. If you are a Death Denier – even if you are in full health and have decades of life expectancy on your side – you might have resisted making a will or any other arrangements. Sometimes I see an almost superstitious resistance to planning.

If this is you, I urge you to consider this kind of forward planning more as an exercise in free will. Given that you will die one day or, as the Death Denier might be prepared to accept, given that most people die one day, you may have some preferences about how that might look for you. The sort of treatment you would choose to have or not have, the kind of company you would prefer, even how you like your cup of tea or coffee. Some of us will unexpectedly be in a situation where we can no longer communicate these things to others – and then what solace for those responsible for our care to have a clear idea of what we like.

Death Defying

To some extent this stance is a cultural issue. For years in the West we have been using phrases like

> "He lost his battle with cancer" or

> "We did everything we could, but we couldn't save her".

In the medical world, death can be seen as the final failure. Yet it is unrealistic to imagine we might all be kept alive indefinitely.

Many of us have seen those hospital dramas where the medical professionals say there's no hope, but somebody fights for better answers and indeed, a new idea is developed which ends up saving the person's life. That is subliminally teaching us that we must fight, that only a defeatist would yield to death.

It might well be, especially if the dying person is older or has been seeing their capabilities decline over time, that they are ready to accept death, but their family are not. They may feel that their duty to their dying loved one is to put all their energy into the battle for life.

"Do whatever you can doctor!"

Yet despite the onus being on medical professionals to preserve life by any means possible, it is interesting to look at the research regarding what they would choose for themselves in a potentially fatal situation.

> *"Most physicians would choose a do-not-resuscitate (DNR) or "no code" status for themselves when they are terminally ill, yet they tend to pursue aggressive, life-prolonging treatment for patients facing the same prognosis, according to a study from the Stanford University School of Medicine." (White, 2014)*

Out of the 2000 doctors surveyed in this research, over 88% said they would not choose DNR. These are the people who know the low success rate of this approach - only about 15% of patients who undergo this treatment will leave the hospital alive, and the traumatic effect on the body of electrical resuscitation.

Our information field is distorted. Many of us might expect these approaches to be as effective as they are on TV since that can be our primary source of the dying experience.

> *"The truth is more depressing than fiction, according to a new study. While medical dramas Grey's Anatomy and House show cardiopulmonary resuscitation saving a patient's life nearly 70 percent of the time, the real immediate survival rate is nearly half that -- around 37 percent."* (California, 2015)

A further distortion is that while getting CPR in a hospital drama gives you a 50% chance of leaving the hospital alive, only 13% are that lucky in real life.

So instead of relying on fiction for information, you may choose to do your own research and make an independent decision.

The dawn of the internet and ready access to oceans of data is a very different world from when my grandparents had absolute faith in The Doctor. In fact, when I asked my doctor about the implications of a recently diagnosed heart murmur, she told me to google it.

Friends who work in this field tell me it is common for patients to come armed with their DIY diagnosis and treatment plan. I'm sure this can be a nuisance at times – though in general a better-informed patient seems like a good thing, so long as they have managed to research their condition in a thorough and balanced way.

Another way to be Death Defying can be to look for a healer. Increased awareness of alternative and complementary therapies, along with rising scepticism about big pharma and allopathic medicine, has created a wealth of options for anybody with the resources to access them. It will usually cost the individual more than the conventional medical route (at least in countries with state-provided healthcare) and it also requires the patient to have the capacity to stand up for their point of view, even while those with different views might be urging them to do otherwise.

Having chosen another path though, they may find that fighting is the antithesis of the approach. Acceptance and forgiveness are more likely to be seen as stages in self-healing as many of these modalities look for the healing to come from within rather than from external sources. So the fight is for the capacity to choose a healthy life rather than a battle against the disease.

Death Loving

I have come across this much less often, but a significant number of people are fascinated by death, near death experiences (NDEs) and life after death. They read about it, talk about it, think about it, and gather with others who feel the same way. Depending on their personality type this can be a profound spiritual or philosophical experience – or a type of anxiety or depression.

Everyone is different and an honest, open-minded conversation with someone is probably enough to see if they need help or support – or if their interest is part of their exploration of the deeper meaning of life.

In certain cases a professional opinion may be helpful if there are concerns that the individual has become obsessed with death, to the detriment of their life experience.

Do bear in mind though, that since the prevailing attitude in modern society is to avoid death, then someone may be misidentified as 'loving death' just because they are prepared to talk about it. They may in fact be taking a healthy interest in this fundamental topic - even though expressing that interest is clearly unacceptable to many people around them. Maybe they are pioneers in rebalancing attitudes in western society. Maybe it is part of their spiritual journey. Maybe it is the inspiration that will lead them to a career supporting those dying or grieving. It is an unusual relationship to have with death, but it is not wrong.

Death Accepting

As each of us approaches death, this position is likely to give us the most chance of peace of mind; being in a state of equanimity as the inevitable moment of death approaches.

Suelin Chen, founder of CAKE, an End-of-Life services company and one of Fortune magazine's 40 under 40 list, asserts:

> *"Addressing death head-on can be empowering and life-affirming. "* *(40 under 40, n.d.)*

The global pandemic (COVID-19) forced many more people to confront their own mortality as death became less something that "Happens to Other People" and more something that could, quite quickly and unexpectedly, "Happen to Me".

Practical acceptance

Accepting death can have many faces. There are the obvious practicalities of getting your affairs in order, making sure you have a will, that someone knows how to access your bank accounts, that the kids / dog / partner / plants will be taken care of when you are gone.

Dealing with probate for my father – who was well organised and with relatively straightforward finances – made me realise just how complex and time consuming these things can be. I imagined how hard that would be for anyone taking over my own affairs, and decided it was time to make clearer records or simplify my affairs.

Dealing with practical issues like this can be an essential prerequisite to the more fundamental work of coming to terms with the idea of our own death.

Emotional / Spiritual acceptance

Many spiritual paths aim for surrender to the concept of the death of our physical body. They may see this life as a test or learning opportunity, a chance to improve the standing of our eternal soul as we journey towards *nirvana* or its equivalent. In most cases they see our earthly body as some kind of temporary flesh suit for our higher self / spirit / soul and that after death we may go to another level of existence, or be reincarnated, or remerge with unity consciousness.

Achieving this mindset can bring great comfort to the dying individual, though it may also cause some friction with those close to them if they do not share their views. Supporting a family around death can involve some arbitration as friends and family try to reconcile their different perspectives.

I have spent some time in Essaouira, a fishing port on the Atlantic coast of Morocco. The boats are flimsy looking wooden affairs and the Atlantic Ocean is huge and opinionated. Like many who work with the earth, with nature, the fishermen are mostly calm and somewhat philosophical. One of the local fishermen explained their approach to me.

> "Every time we go out to fish, usually for 3 or 4 or 5 days, as we each step onto the boat we say, 'I am dead'. We know that the trip is dangerous and that if we get in

trouble, we will be alone. So we accept that this could be the last time we are on dry land.

"And then when the fishing trip is done, and we have made it back safely to port, as we step back on to the land we say, 'I am reborn'."

I find this an extraordinary level of acceptance, especially on such a regular basis. He explained that it means they do not have to be nervous about dying during the trip, because they have already come to terms with it. So if there's a storm, or the boat has a problem they can focus on that instead of on managing their own panic. What sounds at first to be a rather fatalistic or pessimistic attitude is, in fact, uplifting and life enhancing.

Choosing for ourselves

Whichever of these archetypes feels more familiar to you – and knowing that you may see aspects of yourself in all of them, getting clearer about your current relationship with death – or that of someone you are caring for – can be a useful step forward on your journey.

Armed with that insight, let's now look at what might stand between us and the death we would most prefer.

Cleaning up as we go

Most of us have unfinished emotional business. Those fallings out we never cleared up or reconciled. The "I love you" we never said. The confessions that lurk, unspoken, in the back of our hearts and minds.

We can wait for our deathbed to address these. Though I have seen such feelings make it hard for someone to let go, to surrender to death. Clinging in great discomfort to life as they struggle with their unresolved issues.

Or we can choose to clean up as we go.

In general, we go through life assuming we will get at least the average life expectancy. So there's always the chance to put off these uncomfortable interchanges for another day. What if we knew we were to die tomorrow? Is there something we would wish we had done or said?

The bucket list is now a well-known concept, but often the focus on these lists is on physical experiences. Seeing the Grand Canyon. Learning to scuba dive. Driving through Paris in a sports car with the warm wind in our hair.

If you were to write your bucket list in a different way, what might be on it?

Who would you like to forgive?

What would you like to forgive yourself for?

What do you want to get off your chest?

What do you need to say to people close to you?

In the Sacred Death course that I run (see WindsofDiscovery.com for more info) we write letters to at least one person who is important to us. It might be a partner, our children, a parent, a colleague, that girl you were spiteful to 30 years ago. We don't usually send them. The person might no longer be alive. Some letters might be kept aside by participants to be shared after their death. Whatever the outcome, it is an important exercise.

In terms of our own forgiveness, I love this exercise I came across during a retreat – borrowed, I believe, from the 12 steps approach. After a discussion about shame we all had to write a list under the heading "I am ashamed of…". We had to leave a wide margin on the lefthand side of the page.

At first most of us stared dumbly at the blank page, cringing at our memories. Ashamed even to write them down, even though this was a personal exercise that we didn't have to share with anybody else. But then pens started scratching. Most of us speeded up as we went. Once the floodgates were open, and the obvious shame moments written down, other memories came rushing in. Within ten minutes most of us were onto the second sheet of paper.

It was awful. To see that long list and realise how much we were carrying. Memories that had been tucked away in the back of a cupboard for many years, events that maybe we didn't even register at the time, but now felt with that hot itch of shame as we added them to the list.

The next stage was even harder. In the space we had left in the lefthand margin, we had to write "I forgive myself for" in front of every one of these shame events. And then we were invited to read it aloud, either to ourselves or with a partner.
Trying to really feel the forgiveness, the letting go.

It's tough work, but very worthwhile. Ike clearing out the attic or the basement. Even though we couldn't see all that packed away rubbish in our system, it was using up energy by being part of our consciousness (or sub-conscious). Being on our conscience. Better out than in. You might want to try it.

In the Resources section at the end of this book, I share some of the meditations which I have come across in my training both as a shamanic healer and an End-of-Life doula. I have found they can be very helpful.

Preparing ourselves

We cannot rehearse our own death. Unless we have a near death experience, we are likely to arrive at that point without a dress rehearsal – from this life at least. But self-reflection and guided meditations can help us. It can be easier to listen to these things rather than read and try to meditate at the same time, so I have also included links to my YouTube videos if you prefer to sit quietly with your eyes closed and listen to the meditations.

Confronting our death in the way these meditations encourage us to do, can be alarming. Be gentle with yourself, observing your reactions and being at peace with them. You may find you want to repeat the same meditation a few times so your system becomes accustomed to going into this taboo or neglected space in our consciousness.

Remember too how it feels the first time. And have compassion both for yourself in this moment and for others you may work with, who are trying to get used to new information that their death is coming sooner than they expected. Whatever our well-disciplined rational minds may try to say, you are likely to have a visceral response. For some like a punch to the gut, for others like their blood pressure dropping and a fainting feeling, for others a surge of boiling hot rage. Or you may feel none of these things and go instead to mental or spiritual responses.

It is in nature and evolution's interests for us to avoid death where possible. So fear of it is natural. Especially if we have avoided these thoughts for a long time. This is a time to be patient with ourselves. To notice the details of how our body reacts – because there is information there. Journal about your responses. What are your fears, your worries about the last stage of your life? Maybe some of these are things you can do something about now and reduce the burden waiting for each of us at the end.

For instance if you feel a sense of great disappointment that you spent far too much time on things that didn't matter, avoiding your passions and those things that give your life a sense of meaning, then is that something you can adjust now and make different choices for however much of this life you have remaining?

Rather than focusing on regrets and limitations, find space to consider adjustments you can make to liberate your life and, one day, ease your death.

A friend confided in me a few months ago.

> "I regret spending so much of my time worrying about things that may never happen. That usually don't happen. It's such a waste of energy".

I agreed, and gently suggested that at least he was free to change that from now on if he wished to.

He looked, frankly, astonished. Confused.

> "Change it? But it's what I do."

Another friend looked at me when I mentioned my upcoming 60th birthday.

> "Ah if only I was still so young," she said wistfully.

I asked her what her 100-year-old self would say to the 82-year-old she currently was. She had to laugh. We are always the oldest we have ever been. And the youngest we will ever be. We can choose our perspective.

We have many choices, every single day. Just because we always did something one way doesn't mean we are stuck with that behaviour. If considering your death brings you some insights into activities you'd like to drop, behaviours that don't serve you, missed opportunities, then how much better to realise that now, when you might still have the chance to make more aligned choices, rather than wait until you are on your deathbed.

What might you regret on your deathbed? It is so easy to live in the future or to be tethered to the past. Always waiting to start our lives. When we finish this training course… lose that weight… have that baby… find that dream house… get promoted… get the kids through college… have that operation… make those dollars… meet Mr/Ms Right… then before we know it, we are at the end of our life, and we haven't properly started doing what we want.

My personal experience, and that of many of the people attending my courses, has been that thinking clearly and honestly about our own death, making the arrangements we want to make and clarifying the plans we need, frees us to fully live our lives right here, right now. The day we have in our hand at this very moment.

I strongly recommend considering death and your relationship with dying as a life enhancing activity. It can seem counter-intuitive, but I see it happen over and over. And it's supported by lots of other experiences. For instance see elite athlete Elin Kjos's TED talk *My life started when they said it was over*.

There's no need to wait till the last minute to have your epiphany, your flash of inspiration or wisdom. Honour your death in the moment it arrives and honour your life each moment you have until then.

Choosing our journey

So now you have a better idea of your current approach –Death Avoiding, Death Fearing, Death Denying, Death Defying, Death Loving, Death Accepting.

Having increased awareness of our own approach, we are in a better position to start to consider it and make any adjustments which we think will support us on our journey.

It might help to consider how your views have shifted during your life so far. Think back to your childhood, to the belief systems you were raised with, how is that different to now? Maybe you have adopted a religious or spiritual view you weren't brought up in, or dropped the one that you were? Maybe you've had a spiritual awakening or maybe you are disenchanted with the traditions you were raised with. Maybe you have changed dramatically or just made some adjustments.

Do you find you have more equanimity about death as you move and mature through your life - or more fear?

In my own case, I was most afraid of death when I was about ten years old. It was the time of the Cold War, with pamphlets about how to survive a nuclear attack. Even at that age we were dubious about whether the kitchen table would really be good enough protection. And would the stylish new Formica tables in our own homes do less good of a job than our grandmothers' sturdier furniture? We would often discuss the possibility of sudden nuclear attack while we were supposed to be playing at breaktime in the school playground.

And because this was at a convent school, our Number One Concern was how 'clean' our souls would be for the dreaded judgement that awaited us at the pearly gates.

> "We haven't had any terrible things happen to us like the martyrs did, so we won't get into heaven, will we?"

> "I just hope it happens on a day when I've just been to confession, so my soul is clean."

> "Oh yes, I don't want to go to hell!"

> "Surely we haven't been bad enough for that?"

Maybe bad enough for purgatory though, that ambiguous in-between space that we didn't quite understand but didn't think we much liked the sound of either.

> "Maybe if we could confess everything really quickly in the last few minutes that would be alright?"

We could all hear the doubt in her voice, but we hoped against hope that this solution might be available to us.

And then one day, some surprising news entered the conversation.

> "After I went to bed the other night, I heard my uncle telling my mum there's no such thing as hell!"

Collective gasp of astonishment and relief. If that were true it would change everything. We hardly dared hope that we had all just got off the hook.

Interestingly, we never talked about the loss of our human life at such a young age, we were just afraid of what the next life had in store.

That was also the age when I would lie awake at night thinking of all the ways I might die (all painful and terrifying, all based on what I had seen on TV and films, as at that point I didn't know any actual people who had died). I would conclude there was no good way to go and dread the day.

It was a grim prospect. And I'm very glad that I no longer feel that way. A combination of many more years of life, a broader perspective, and my trainings as an End-of-Life doula and in using shamanic healing techniques have all shifted my view.

My hope with this book is that your view might shift a little too. To a more comfortable place where you might be more at peace with the concept of death. Firstly your own, and then by association, that of others. The more of us can shift to this position the better able we will be, as a society, to handle the inevitable deaths in our lives with more grace and compassion.

The importance of Self Care

While you are reading this book, there may be times when you feel triggered by the content. Long-forgotten memories and emotions will come up for healing. This is all a valuable part of your journey.

It is also a useful opportunity to practice self-care – an essential part of your death journey, especially when you are accompanying somebody else through their death.

All too often we see that those caring for a dying person get themselves into an unsustainable role. They can end up trying to be everything for the other person – friend, priest, nurse, confidant, counsellor, financial adviser… I have seen End-of-Life doulas become exhausted as they accept all sorts of practical aspects of their client's life, well beyond their remit – from walking the dog to getting the boiler mended. We aim to be there for people, but not to create an unsustainable dependency.

Of course it is natural to wish to help someone. And they are dying after all, so we might feel that our own needs cannot possibly compete with that. We might be motivated by survivor guilt or kindness but it's always important to maintain perspective.

Again and again we must gently remind ourselves that we can only serve others if we are in the right state ourselves. Death is an unpredictable business, and while maintaining a 24-hour vigil may be possible for a few days, what if it goes on for weeks or months as the dying person confounds medical predictions and lives for much longer than expected?

Being at the bedside at the moment of death can feel like the most important thing of all. Yet research shows that someone will often choose the very moment when nobody is in the room to slip away.

I saw this quote on allnurses.com, a community website for nurses:

> *I don't work in hospice, but a friend of mine does and she's seen this happen several times. A patient will be circling the drain, the family stays and stays and stays, and the minute they leave for two minutes, the patient dies. The family ends up distraught and feeling guilty.*

The responses on that website, from registered nurses and hospice workers, confirm the frequency of this. We need to know, as a society, that this is a common occurrence and does not need to create a feeling of shame of failure.

Put yourself in the shoes of the dying person for a moment. While you are sad about losing them, and all the possibilities of your future together, remember that they are losing not only you, but every other person they know, every dream, every plan they had for the future, every taste and touch and smell. They are letting go of a lot more than anyone else at their bedside and they may just need a private moment to come to terms with that. They might need to be alone to find the courage to step out of this life.

If you talk to hospice workers or spend time in any of the death and grief chatrooms, you will often hear of this happening. It is not a failure on the part of the people spending time with their loved ones in the last days and hours. They have been there for some of the journey and that is a precious experience. Maybe more importantly they have allowed their loved one to leave, at a moment of their choosing.

So one aspect of self-care is the need to look after ourselves, so we are in good shape to look after the needs of others.

Understanding your own self-care

On my Sacred Death course I ask my students to keep a self-care diary. There are two columns – helpful self-care actions and unhelpful ones. The distinction between the two is mostly about how well it serves your needs.

Our unhelpful self-care actions are often semi-automatic. Reaching for the wine bottle or cigarette packet. Getting lost in social media or distracting ourselves with Netflix. The clue that they are unhelpful is your level of consciousness while you are doing them. Are you in your power, in your sovereignty when you make these choices, or do you feel more like they are choosing you?

There's a difference between creating a sanctuary for yourself and slowly savouring two or three squares of chocolate, relishing the flavour and texture, and nourishing yourself with this personal time – versus scoffing a couple of Mars bars without even noticing and feeling sick or guilty afterwards.

Our nervous system reaches out for some things because they temporarily numb the pain. But it's worth considering if they really make you feel better. Do they give you energy? Peace? Comfort? Now you've bought that new pair of summer sandals and the short-lived hit of pressing the buy button is over, do you really feel in a better place? Was it worth it?

Other options might require a bit more intention or self-discipline. … options like going for a walk in nature, meditating, joining a yoga class, reading a thought-provoking or soothing book, cooking a healthy meal. They take more effort, but it's worth noticing for yourself if they help you more.

The idea of the self-care diary is just to observe our own patterns. What do we reach for and how does it make us feel? Is a bubble bath great when we are frazzled but no use if we need clarity? The more we understand our own needs and responses, the better we can look after ourselves.

It is also important to be aware of the emotional aspect of self-care. A lot will be coming up for you as you go through this book or sit at the bedside of someone who is dying or confront the idea of your own death. It's important to make sure we process those feelings – acknowledging and letting them flow through us – so they don't get stuck in our system and cause us illness or distress. Check in with yourself now and then to assess your level of feeling at ease – or not. And act sooner rather than later.

What are your warning signs that you are running risks with your self-care? Do you start to get a headache? A rash? Have trouble sleeping? Lose your appetite or gorge on snacks? We all have different ways of responding and again it is good to know ourselves. The earlier we can pick up on these symptoms, maybe while they are still just whispers, the less need for them to develop into shouts or more fundamental health problems.

Self-care Exercise

Keep a self-care diary for a week. Have three categories that you complete each day:

1. Symptoms of lack of self-care (eg headache, cravings, sleeplessness, snapping at people)
2. Unhelpful self-care actions (eg compulsive drinking, smoking, social media, binge-watching Netflix… activities

      that we do almost on automatic pilot without noticing each
      moment)
3. Helpful self-care (eg cooking, sharing feelings with a wise
      friend, journaling, observing nature, exercise)

Sometimes you might notice that the same activity can fall into helpful or unhelpful depending on how you approach it. In general the more conscious you are the better. You don't need to be sitting cross legged on a yoga mat to meditate or support your sense of inner peace. It might be achieved by doing the washing up if you approach the task with conscious mindfulness and intention.

Just write down everything you think is relevant and then review it at the end of the week. Without judgement. So often students come to my class after this exercise and start by either beating themselves up for not completing it every day or making self-deprecating comments about themselves and their observations.

See if instead you can review your self-care diary with an attitude of self-care. With kindness. With love. Be gentle with yourself. What are some seeds of good habits that you might choose to nurture? How does being more aware of your warning signs help you act earlier - before you have a migraine or a fight with your partner? How can you support yourself when you have urges for unhelpful self-care that you maybe now realise is not caring for yourself at all?

Start having conversations with friends about self-care. Maybe you will pick up some interesting ideas. Someone who always writes a limerick, finding the comedy in their stressful situation. Another who lays the table with the best crockery and glassware and has a lovely dinner, even though she is eating alone. A third who always finds something among her possessions to give away when she is feeling overwhelmed. There are as many options as there are humans. Someone might inspire you and help you on this journey. Or you might help them.

At the very least you will have raised your awareness – and maybe that of your friends too. First put attention on yourself so you can be of more help to others. Be a new kind of First Responder.

In the Building Presence exercise in Section 3, we will be looking at the second and third stages of this process of creating the right state to support someone who is dying or grieving. As well as this first stage of putting attention on ourselves, we also see how to put attention on the space around us and thirdly on the person we want to support.

Switching exercise

In my classes I teach a simple process called switching, shared with me by the amazing organisation Capacitar International (Capacitar international, n.d.) who teach trauma release first aid techniques in humanitarian crises all over the world. You can see the switching technique on YouTube, demonstrated in this video by Clare Cable of QNI Scotland.

- Start by crossing your ankles, the left one over the right.
- Then stretch your arms out in front of you and cross right over left at the elbows.
- Turn your hands so your palms face each other and clasp your hands.
- Bring your clasped hands down and under until they reach your breastbone, resting your knuckles there and letting your elbows relax against your body.
- Maintain this posture in a relaxed way, aware of your heartbeat, of your sense of self, anchored there.

Ideally, use this position whenever you are listening to somebody else share their troubles. It will support you in being able to hold compassionate presence for them while also reminding your own nervous system that this is somebody else's story. You can witness their pain and absolutely be there for them - without having to feel it directly or risk being dragged down until you are no longer able to help them. This is especially important if you are regularly working with people who are dying or in pain or trauma and need to maintain a healthy balance within your own nervous system.

When I am holding Trauma Release or Grief Circles, I have people sit in this position as we share stories. Participants report that it helps them maintain peace and equanimity without any loss of compassion or empathy for the person who is sharing. In fact it increases their capacity as they can feel for the other person without being overwhelmed by the fear of risking their own wellbeing.

In day-to-day situations, adopting this position could feel awkward – in which case do it for a few minutes before an interaction that could be difficult, and as soon as you have a moment of privacy during or after the conversation. Even if that means excusing yourself for an otherwise unnecessary trip to the bathroom so you can sit in this position until you restabilise and can return to the other person in a more supportive state.

I have taught this technique around the world and notice some common reactions - a sigh of relief, a slight smile, a relaxing of the shoulders. It might feel a little strange at first but maintaining your own sense of well-being is vital if you want to be of service to others.

Section 3: Society and death

Letting go of preconceptions

Our death – or the death of someone close to us, does not exist in isolation. We have been on the receiving end of messaging around death since the day we were born. When we talk about decolonising death, we are referring to bringing visibility to these influences – some subtle, some legal, some cultural – so that we can examine them with open eyes and decides where we go from here.

Letting Go Exercise

Take a moment to list the messages you have received during your life so far. From your parents, your teachers, religious leaders, gurus, friends. From the books you have read and the films you watched. From the news cycle and social media.

Write the list as quickly and honestly as you can, not pausing to consider if these views were right or wrong, just acknowledging them.

How many are positive? How many are empowering? How many bring you a sense of peace?

It's likely that your answer is not many, unless you grew up in an ashram.

Now we have exposed these views though, we can let them go. Thank them for helping clarify our thoughts and let them go. Now let's be more alert to the views we choose to have, the ones that we think might be more helpful to ourselves and others.

Developing our own perspective

I'm going to share a part of my own journey from received views – the ones I was taught by my family, religion, society - towards developing my own view. You are on your own journey from what you were exposed to, towards what you choose. Your views may or may not share some aspects with mine. The important thing is that they are the views from your own heart.

After giving birth myself, I was suddenly struck by how unrealistic most birth scenes in films and TV are. The drama, the panic, the things going wrong, the sheer speed from first contraction or waters breaking were all at odds with my own beautiful experience of three gentle home deliveries with a birthing pool and the tender-strong support of amazing midwives.

I know I was lucky and that others are not. Yet many births do just proceed as expected. So why not expect a beautiful sacred moment. Childbirth doesn't need to be a dreadful experience. Or a medical-led event. I was very happy in my own home with fresh air, scented candles, my favourite music and the people I wanted to be there. No sensory overload of bright lights, clanging metal, busy strangers or unpleasant smells. I also found it deeply empowering to feel I was leading the process. Or rather that I was letting my body lead the process. A natural timeline unhampered by rotas, shift changes or a sense of losing control.

From then on, it has seemed a shame to me that birth is rarely shown to be like this. And since in the West we are not usually birthing at home, with the children and family nearby, many of us will not have been present at a birth until we find ourselves experiencing it first-hand. Small wonder that fear of birth is so prevalent:

> *"Studies suggest that at least 50% of women experience fear about labour and delivery at some point during pregnancy." (Dr. Jasmine Shaikh, 2022)*

How might it be if we lived in a world where we had already seen our sisters and neighbours give birth? Where we knew that – as recorded by Johns Hopkins Medicine - over 90% of pregnancies and births don't have complications and those that do are:

> *"Mostly manageable with good pre-natal care".*
> *(Medicine, 2021).*

A world where we had good information about the essential oils or foods or sounds that would support our bodies to be in alignment and do what they already know how to do? Where we let our body choose a birthing position rather than just do as we are told based on convenience for the professionals?

As Robin Lim, world famous midwife and champion of empowering birth explained to me recently:

> "We need to decolonise birth."

To organise around the diverse needs of women and communities, rather than a convenient process for the medical and legal system.

The phrase struck home, and I realised that I want to do the same – to decolonise death. To reclaim it and make it about the people experiencing it, not the establishment.

When I applied for the Living Well Dying Well End-of-Life doula course, it struck me that my interest in learning more about being with people on their death journey was very similar to my reasons for wanting a home birth.

I felt then – and feel more and more with experience, that death, like birth, is a sacred moment. That the beginning – or end – of someone's life is far more than a medical situation to be managed. These are arguably the two most important moments of our current human lives. The beginning and the ending. The two moments of transition from wherever we believe we came to wherever we believe we go after leaving this mortal, physical body.

Sacred Birth and Sacred Death

You don't need to be religious or spiritual to have a sense of the sacredness of the moment of birth or death. The wonder of life. The wonder of nature. It touches us deeply.

One of the inspiring voices in this field is Elisabeth Kübler-Ross. Check out her book in the Resources section of this book. In one she co-wrote with David Kessler; they comment on the trade-off we have between fear and love:

> *"If we're in fear, we are not in a place of love. When we're in a place of love, we cannot be in a place of fear. Can you think of a time when you've been in both love and fear? It's impossible." (Kessler, 2014)*

So when the information we receive is mostly telling us to fear birth, and fear death (and in between, fear life) how much might that cripple our ability to feel love?

In our own moments of being born and dying what could we want more than love? We are journeying alone through that birth passage or death experience, and to feel love around us would surely give us more strength and courage for the journey.

We can see how mother-to-be feeling fear as her primary state might have a different birth. She would be less relaxed, experience more pain and have stress hormones in her system that might transmit to her baby. There is a clear physical connection as described in this research project in the Journal of Maternal and Child Health.

> *Delivery pain increases with higher anxiety. Anxiety associated with delivery pain, stress, and coping mechanism... if these symptoms are not well-managed, they can cause low birth weight, prematurity, prolonged labour, and postpartum depression. (Shofia Maharani Khoirun Nisa, 2018)*

And of course we are all energetically connected. So both the mother and the baby will also be affected by the feelings of the other people in the room. Maybe the nurse has a personal crisis she is dealing with. Maybe the father-to-be is a seething mass of doubts and worries. Or, if they are lucky, maybe the atmosphere can support love, not fear.

Likewise at the deathbed. It is such a crucible of human emotion, such an intense experience, that a lot will be going on energetically. The dying person will have their own responses. Hopes and fears, regrets and griefs. And so too will all the other people involved. Every one of us is a complex mix of experiences, tendencies, ideas and feelings. The child about to lose a parent, the man about to lose the love of his life, the support staff in the room with their own complex lives hovering in the back of their minds. All this emotional energy is in the room and the most supportive thing we can do is channel love rather than feed fear. But how?

Building Presence Exercise

I recommend a 3-step process to my students. It can be counter intuitive at first since our tendency is to jump into putting all our attention on to the other person. We think that's our job. But it's important that we are in the right state ourselves before doing that, so we must start within.

Step One: Yourself

We start with ourselves (be a First Responder to your own needs).

Make sure your feet are firmly grounded. Breathe gently into your own body. Scan your body for tension and discomfort. Are you scrunching up your face? Hunching your shoulders? Clenching your fists? Where are the emotions creating physical feelings in your body? Breathe into any physical tension you encounter, to soften it.

Then notice where your emotional self is at right now. Accept yourself exactly as you are. Quiet the voices telling you how you *should* be, how you are falling short, how you are failing. That is just your fear talking. And we want to be filled with love, so it is necessary to find the strength to step away from fear. Love and accept yourself exactly as you are. You are here. You hope and intend to support others.

Feel your own reactions. Observe them, accept them, and let them go as much as you can. Breathe into these emotions, sending them love and tenderness. Loosen your grip on them. Let them float away.

Step Two: The space

Now expand your awareness to the room. The space where this situation is happening. Be aware of the temperature of the air. Any breeze on your skin. The feel of the floor beneath your feet or the chair you are sitting on. The sounds and smells. The colours. Let your energy expand to every corner of the room so you can hold the maximum amount of space for the dying or grieving person who you want to support.

Step Three: The other person

Only when you feel as secure as you can today with steps 1 and 2, bring your attention to the other person.

What can you feel about them, without needing to ask any questions. How are their eyes? The colour of their skin? Their breathing? Do they seem too hot or cold? Agitated? Calm? Absent? Are they moving at all? Twitching? Fidgeting? Trembling? Or totally still?

What can you detect about their energy field? You don't need to believe you have psychic powers – or even believe in psychic powers - to assess their energy field. We do it all the time, judging when people are angry or loving or uninterested. Have the feeling that you are holding space for them and their energy field. All aspects of their being. Their physical state, their state of mind, their mood, their soul or higher self - if that feels right to you. All is valid. All is welcome. They are here. You and they are here together in this experience.

You are now holding space, offering compassionate presence. Breathe into it. Accept them exactly as they are. Just as you accept yourself exactly as you are. We are all perfect for this moment of our lives. We might be learning or expanding or being at peace. It's all ok. All we must do is be fully present, with acceptance.

Holding space

> *"We have to become still in the midst of the turmoil so*
> *we can observe clearly how our actions and the*
> *actions of others, past and present, fit together in the*
> *tapestry of life. In the timeless instant when we stop*
> *moving and simply witness the moment, the dust*
> *settles, and the big picture emerges." (Villoldo, 2018)*

If you are sitting with someone who is dying you may be there for
minutes – or hours. It is unlikely you will be able to hold this sense
of compassionate presence consistently for the whole time. Again,
be gentle with yourself. If your stomach is rumbling it is natural
that you start wondering about food – how and what you can eat.
Or in the peace of the moment your mind can wander to
memories, to your own plans, to current concerns in your life.

We are humans with wandering minds. An essential aspect of our
evolution. And as soon as you notice and want to bring yourself
back to the here and now, as often as you need to, just follow the
same three steps described above:

1. **Bring your attention to yourself**. Feet flat on the floor.
    Spine straight. Breathe deep into your lower belly. Feel
    your rooted connection to the earth and the spaciousness
    above your head. Notice where you are feeling physical or
    emotional discomfort and send love and breath there.
2. **Feel the space around you**. Extend your energy, your aura,
    your awareness, to the corners of the room or the space you
    are in. Take in the temperature, the breeze, the sounds.
    Occupy the space so you are surrounding the dying
    person.
3. **Focus on the dying person**. Pay attention to their
    breathing. Their skin. Their energy field (even if you
    believe that you can't see or feel that, imagine that you

can). Where do they need most support? Where might they need soothing? Or strengthening?

My own experience has been that the first five minutes of holding space in this way are the hardest. We are so used to living busy lives, dashing from one task to the next, while reviewing the previous one and planning for future ones. We have become so used to busy-ness – that it has become a measure of validity in the world.

"Hi, how're you doing?"

"Oh you know, keeping busy."

"Yes! Me too. It never stops, does it?"

And of course it won't ever stop, our work and family and community will take everything we offer. It is only us who can stop. Pause. Breathe. Reflect.

Slowing down

My life was overly busy for 30 years. Career, kids, community work, hobbies, studies. So much so that when I stopped to admire a cosy armchair while walking with my mother through a furniture store, she exclaimed: "I don't know why you're interested in that. You never sit down!"

It has been a revelation to me that doing less can mean achieving more. Of course it is easier now anyway because I am at a different life stage, but I wonder if I could have been doing less all along.

You've probably noticed if you check your messages after a while away from your devices, that some of the problems you were told about but didn't read earlier on, have solved themselves by the time you've found out about them. None of us have sole responsibility for the whole world, even if it can sometimes feel like that.

So one of the gifts for you in working with the dying might be the deep sense of peace you find in these hours sitting in semi-darkness by the bedside. Not scrolling through your phone, not tidying up, not trying to make anything happen. Sitting in the infinite spaciousness and timelessness of the days and hours approaching death. Maybe absorbing some of the perspective of the dying person.

Living in Bali for a few years has given me great insights into this states. The first time I was here for NYEPI (Balinese New Year) I couldn't imagine how I would cope with their Day of Silence. Local friends had explained it to me. No electricity, internet or phones, no work, cooking, or leaving the house. Not even a candle after sunset. A day of contemplation. It sounded terrifying to me. But also intriguing. A worthy challenge.

That first NYEPI, it rained non-stop all day. I wondered how I would fill the hours. Just me and a bowl of fruit and my thoughts. I sat on my porch steps wondering what to do. Watching the rain. Observing the droplets gathering in a leaf until they were too heavy to stay there and rolled slowly down its central line, dropping off the tip and scattering on the ground beneath. The leaf sprang back up, relieved of the weight of the drop of water. I watched it again. The random patter of raindrops, some bouncing straight off the leaf, others moving to the gathering point at the end. The growing of that central drop of rainwater and then the slow slide as the water rolled off the tip and the leaf sprang back.

An hour passed. I would not have thought it possible. Something of the stillness of the whole island entered my bloodstream. The lack of planes, traffic, chatter, pressure to DO. The bird song was more prominent. The rain continued. The focus was on BEING.

I watched some ants in their complicated housekeeping operations. One picked up a large crumb. Then dropped its awkward load. It picked it up a different way, then dropped it again. The third way worked, and it managed to carry the crumb for ten or fifteen centimetres before it dropped it.

Tirelessly it continued like that, every time trying the same three different holds in the same order. No learning then? Interesting. In our anthropomorphism of ants don't we tend to assume more intelligence? What if these creatures' undeniable achievements are merely the product of diligence, persistence, never feeling like they've had enough and abandoning the idea? Eventually the ant would get the crumb to its destination. It might take hours. I envied its determination even as I was frustrated by its lack of efficiency.

The day passed. Observing minutiae. Breathing, yoga, meditation, fruit. The sun set some time after 6pm and with no light allowed, there seemed little option but to stare at the stars (even more beautiful than usual because of the complete lack of light on the island) then go to bed. A crash course in slowing down. In learning how to not always be doing something.

And what beautiful preparation for death and death work. What an insight into a different state, where tasks and distractions become irrelevant.

So we practice, we learn, and we develop our capacity to hold compassionate presence. Not only at the deathbed but in many stressful moments of life. When you lose your job, or your friend's partner leaves them, or you watch shocking news events unfold on your screen. Everything we learn about death also helps us in our life.

Controversial deaths

Sadly, society doesn't treat all deaths as equal. Some deaths elicit a universal response of sympathy, others invoke a more pragmatic response or even a sense that the death or the bereaved person are not worthy of a kind offer of support.

Even with sympathetic responses there might be a hint of a scale. Consider the different reactions you might get to these two statements.

"Oh well, he was 80. You know, had a good innings…"

"And she was only six. Poor little thing."

It is true that the implications of some deaths are certainly more challenging – maybe a dying parent is leaving young children behind. Maybe the political or community leader, the artist or guru seem irreplaceable. But every death deserves a respectful response.

And then there are the more complex reactions generated by deaths involving suicide, overdoses or euthanasia, and the judgment and shame that can surround abortion or miscarriages.

And then how do people feel about murderers on death row? It is no great surprise that lack of sympathy for those who are awaiting execution is correlated to more generalised racial resentment, since black Americans are six times more likely to end up in this situation (Death Penalty Demographics, 2023)

> *Beliefs about race, especially racial resentment, are key predictors of public support for capital punishment and punitiveness generally (Kellie R. Hannan, 2022)*

These deaths can carry stigma, a sense of guilt for some, a feeling of failure. Society has developed a view of these deaths – and different cultures, religions and lifestyle choices can generate semi-automatic responses that don't pay much attention to the nuances and hidden complexities of every story.

Let's consider in more depth how these more controversial deaths might also benefit from the light of compassion.

I have experienced some of these complexities and share the stories of those involved to bring some light and life to the terms. The names have been changed to protect those involved. The more we know about the individual and their situation, the harder it is to judge. The less clearcut the decision seems. When the urge to judge arises in us - which of course it always will since we are humans with our own set of experiences, biases and beliefs - I find it helps to remember there is always a lot we don't know.

Death by Suicide

Although suicide is no longer illegal in many Western countries, there is still stigma. And according to the website Understanding Suicide, in 25 countries it is outlawed, with a further 20 countries following Islamic or Sharia law which usually means jailtime for attempted suicide. (Mishara, 2016)

Even in countries where it is allowed, it is common to talk of "committing suicide" as though it were still a criminal act. As well as the known 800,000 people a year who choose this option, there will be many more where data is not reliably gathered, where stigma or fear of repercussions, including legal recourse, mean the family hide the real cause of death.

The parents or partner of someone who has chosen to kill themselves will have to deal with their own grief as well as judgment from outsiders and possible negative practical consequences such as impact on life insurance pay-outs. Not to mention the emotional trauma that comes from any sudden death.

Suicide can be seen as an exercise in free will. A personal choice. Although suicide rates have been declining for ten years, they are still about 30% higher than 20 years ago. We may think of this as a rich country problem, but according to WHO, three quarters of the deaths by suicide each year are in low- and middle-income countries. It is significantly more common for men than women and has shifted over time from being most likely in middle aged men to being more evenly spread across all ages.

There were alarming media warnings that the COVID-19 pandemic would fuel a significant increase in suicides. This has been challenged as irresponsible by ICSPRC (International COVID-19 Suicide Prevention Research Collaboration) and is not supported by data.

> *"There is a large body of research literature documenting the potentially harmful effects of news reporting of suicide deaths on population suicide rates. Concerning aspects of reporting include description of suicide methods, sensational headlines, and excessive reporting – these can lead to suicidal behaviour among vulnerable people." (Tandon, 2021)*

Let us just be mindful that this is a complex topic. Suicide is often a multi-factor response rather than driven by a single cause. Suspending judgment and offering compassion might be the best we can do.

Tania's story

Tania had a fraught childhood in Brazil. Raised by her grandparents she was led to believe she was their only child. Then when she was 12 years old and collecting fruit from nearby trees, a couple drove up to the house where she lived, introduced themselves as her real parents and took her "home".

This was a brutal and unexpected change in her life. And as a black girl raised by black grandparents, she was confused to see that her mother and two of her siblings were white.

She struggled to establish a place for herself in the family. Her older brothers resented her return, taunting her and then sexually abusing her. She longed for her happy childhood living in the rainforest with her grandparents.

At the age of 14, after two years of misery, Tania ran away and hitched a lift to the nearest town. She had no money, little education and no plan, so she was relieved when someone offered her work as a maid. They seemed like a nice family, so she wasn't at all prepared, or sure what to do, when the man of the house started insisting on having sex with her when his wife and children were out.

She ran away again and eventually found work in another city. She was traumatised, vulnerable and lonely, so when she was picked up by Jehovah's Witnesses and taken to their church she was captivated. At last people seemed to be treating her with love and kindness. She felt like she belonged. Maybe this was the nurturing family she longed for.

Despite these difficulties in her early life, Tania always imagined that one day she would have a husband and children of her own instead of looking after other people's. In preparation for this she worked hard and gradually got better positions. She improved her literacy and one of her employers paid for her to have English classes and learn tailoring. She started to supplement her income making suits and wedding dresses for friends.

Then at the age of 35, with the discovery of many large cysts in her reproductive system she had a full hysterectomy, as recommended by her doctor. The night before the operation she spent hours painting her fingernails and toenails.

"So I will look nice in my coffin" she explained.

She really didn't expect to survive the operation and was a little startled to wake up afterwards and start her convalescence.

By this time she was working with a British family and, needing a fresh start, she was glad she was able to move back to the UK with them. As their children grew, she had more spare time. Despite continuing to be part of the Jehovah's Witness community she decided she was ready for a boyfriend.

The family helped Tania set up a dating profile and she soon found herself busy with many offers of dates. Her church community were not impressed though, and she was devastated when they suspended her from participating in services for 12 months because she had been on unchaperoned dates and had physical contact with a man. Polishing off a bottle of wine she'd been given as a gift she became suicidal and only survived when security in the building where she lived intervened, and a doctor was called to sedate her.

The internet dating continued, and she met, then married David, a gentle soul who was dazzled by her good looks and high spirits. She didn't tell him about her troubled childhood, nor about the severe bouts of depression (she had undiagnosed bipolar disorder and didn't want any support in managing her mood swings). She also didn't mention the earlier suicide attempt.

Tania tried to settle into this new life - her nice house, nice car and nice husband. For the first time she had security and status. Nobody knew about her past. But after a while, the darkness returned, and the nice husband had no idea how to help her. Despite being referred to counselling support by friends and by her mentor, she refused to discuss her problems with anybody. The shame she already felt about what had happened to her, compounded by the Jehovah's Witness trial ran too deep.

After 3 years of marriage, David came downstairs one morning to find Tania had killed herself with a kitchen knife. Her note read:

"I'm sorry I couldn't be happy".

Take a moment to breathe and let Tania's story settle in. It is not an easy one. Consider how you are feeling right now about this true story. How has it triggered you? Maybe there are echoes for you around abuse, abandonment, depression or suicide. Be kind to yourself while you process these reactions. First show yourself compassion and then consider Tania and David with compassion. It can help to ask yourself questions about the situation to process the story.

- Is suicide ever an acceptable option?
- How can David come to terms with what has happened?
- What might have made a difference?
- Who is to blame?

Maybe you have known others in similar situations. Would anything have changed the outcome?

With the benefit of a bit more information, what some were heard to judge as inexcusable or ungrateful, starts to make more sense.

> "She had everything she wanted, she had nothing to complain about. What was she thinking?"

We see a little of the rich tapestry of events that makes up each person, creating an internal logic for their actions that might bear no relation to our own. But is no less valid. It is hard enough to understand our own inner world – what chance have we of grasping somebody else's?

Abortion and termination

Abortion – especially given the 2022 changes in legislation in the USA – continues to be a divisive topic and can be presented, by those not in favour, as a cowardly or heartlessly convenient way out of a tricky situation.

The truth of course is usually far more complex. The circumstances of the conception, the nature of the relationship, the parenting experience the pregnant woman has received herself, her perceived capability of raising a child, the likely family reaction, the country context… so many things can be part of the story and it is unlikely to be a casual choice.

When we are working with a dying person, we might ask them about their family tree (see Section 5 for more on this). Spending time with a person talking about their family provides a lot of insight into current relationships, past wounds and important connections. We also ask – in confidence of course - about miscarriages and abortions on that family tree. Sometimes these stories have never been shared with anyone and it can bring the dying person peace to confide in an objective, supportive third party.

When I do shamanic healing with a client, I sometimes find there are still energetic connections to these unborn children. As I release these connections it can help the person to die more peacefully. See more in the Section 8 about this aspect of death work.

As an example of some of the complex issues that can arise around terminations, let us spend some time considering Silvia's story.

Silvia's story

Silvia is 22 years old when and working long hours managing a busy boutique in London. She a month ago she ended a four-month relationship with Leon and wants no more to do with him. She has lost a lot of weight lately and attributes her lack of menstruation to this.

However, she has recently discovered she is pregnant. She had an abortion a few years earlier without telling anyone. This time though she feels differently. She has a strong urge to keep the baby. She realises it's only fair to tell her ex, Leon, but he takes it badly. He says he is too young at 28 to be a father. He doesn't want the responsibility. He thinks she should definitely have an abortion.

Silvia decides to confide in her mother, Francesca. She knows Francesca would never dream of having an abortion herself, but her mother is also a feminist, so pro-choice in principle. Plus Silvia doesn't feel like there is anyone else she can turn to. None of her friends have children yet and she is pretty sure they would think an abortion is the obvious choice. She wants more space to think things through. To work out why she already feels attached to this baby.

Francesca is shocked to hear Sylvia's news but is glad her daughter has confided in her. She does her best to listen openly, asking questions and exploring options. She is surprised how emotionally attached she feels to her potential grandchild from the very first mention of the baby, but she keeps her feelings to herself as she doesn't want to sway Silvia's decision.

The situation is further complicated by Silvia's mental health condition which requires regular meetings with her support team. She mentions the pregnancy to her psychiatrist at her next monthly check up. He immediately refers her to the specialist team who look after women with mental health problems who are also expecting a baby. Silvia is somewhat reassured by the support, but it also raises new concerns for her. She starts to question if she is fit to be a mother. There seems to be a mild sense of panic in the psychiatrist's reaction.

Francesca tries to remain neutral but also points out to Silvia that if she wants to keep the baby, she can move back home, and the whole family can support her.

> "You don't need to do this on your own. We can manage between us."

Meanwhile the unwanted boyfriend Leon returns, full of remorse and carrying a teddy and first set of clothes for his "child". He has decided he wants the baby now. And he wants Silvia. He wants to make a family.

Silvia is appalled. She thought she had got rid of him and now here he is back again. She is torn. In some ways she wants the baby, but she certainly doesn't want him in her life. Yet as the father she guesses he probably has rights too. Why had she even told him? she challenges herself. And how can she keep the baby without also having to deal with him?

At the next psychiatric appointment, Francesca goes along too. The team are keen for Silvia to decide, now she is 16 weeks pregnant, and time is running out for the abortion option. Nobody seems to have clarity about next steps.

Francesca has never been a fan of the unimaginative and impersonal therapist, but her heart breaks when he clumsily points out to her horrified daughter,

> "Well obviously you won't be allowed to breastfeed. The baby would be affected by your schizophrenia drugs. You can probably bottle-feed it though if someone is supervising you".

Before Francesca has gathered her wits enough to stop him, he goes on to say,

> "Obviously we'd have to make sure you were never alone with the baby. You might think it was an alien and kill it! Haha"

Somehow Silvia maintains her composure in his office, but as they walk to the car after the appointment, she starts sobbing and words tumble out of her.

> "I'll never be a fit mother! You heard them. I'd probably kill the baby. It's too much of a risk. And even if I do, I can't breastfeed it. I won't be a proper mother. And I haven't got any money and I work long hours and…"

Francesca still believes that as a family they could find a way to make it work. Though at the back of her mind she is aware that she has been looking forward to the day when she no longer has children of her own and can have more freedom. This would take her right back to the start. All those sleepless nights and coaxing out of bed into school uniform. The unfed rabbits and un-walked dogs – would it be all of that all over again?

Her over-riding feeling though is love – for her daughter and for her potential grandchild. And that knocks all the practical, rational concerns out of the window. She holds her daughter, comforting and reassuring her.

What does this situation bring up for you? Maybe you have faced similar dilemmas. Maybe you live in a country where abortion is illegal (25 countries) or restricted (a further 50 countries) (Barry, 2022)

In many countries, unwed mothers are subjected to stigma and unwanted babies may put existing family members at risk as limited resources are spread across one more mouth to feed. So the stakes increase – a back street abortion with the associated risks or a life of being a derided outsider.

This is a widespread situation. According to the Guttmacher Institute:

- Unintended pregnancy and abortion are experiences shared by people around the world. These reproductive health outcomes occur irrespective of country income level, region or the legal status of abortion.
- Roughly 121 million unintended pregnancies occurred each year between 2015 and 2019.
- Of these unintended pregnancies, 61% ended in abortion. This translates to 73 million abortions per year. (Guttmacher.org, 2022)

So 73 million women a year are making this choice – and probably a good deal more considering it and then making a different decision. This rate is highest in North Africa and the Middle East – lowest in the Global North and Australia. Factors that reduce abortion rates include access to alternative ways to control fertility and pregnancy, increased levels of female literacy and women's empowerment. Unintended pregnancy rates are three times as high in low-income countries.

Miscarriage

Another type of death that can invoke complicated reactions are miscarriages. When we raise this in grief circles or when working with the dying, it is surprising how many unshared miscarriages women have experienced. For all kinds of reasons they haven't disclosed the pregnancy to anyone before the miscarriage takes place.

So when miscarriage does occur, they might just brush it aside, or feel ashamed – that they somehow failed as a mother – or be relieved if the pregnancy was not planned, then maybe guilty about that feeling of relief.

In my own case I was overly swayed by the relief of the father that there wasn't going to be a new baby to deal with – and buried my own feelings for years until the End-of-Life doula training encouraged me to face my grief.

For women and couples who struggle with fertility, maybe never carrying a pregnancy to term, the grief can be just as real as for a human who has made it to birth. We all grieve differently and within a couple this difference in responses may put unbearable strain on the relationship.

Often societal norms don't encourage openness about miscarriages, especially if there is any sense of judgement about the way the mother has acted during the pregnancy. She may not feel she can share openly, and this will complicate her grief process.

I was interested to discover that in Bali, there are special ceremonies for children lost during pregnancy or birth. It is believed that if these are not carried out then the soul of the unborn child will not be able to move on in its journey – or be reincarnated.

As I teach on my Sacred Death course though, it is never too late. I carried out a ceremony for my own three miscarriages ten years after the last one. It was still beautiful and meaningful. I have also been called to houses to help release souls of these unborn children that have not detached and are still in the space, sometimes causing problems for the current residents.

If you or your partner have had a miscarriage and feel now that you could honour and grieve that event more clearly, then I encourage you to do so. If you follow a religion, you may already have access to a ceremony or form of words that has meaning for you. If not, then follow your instincts and create something that feels right. I know people who have named their child, sung lullabies, floated flowers down the river, planted a tree… there are lots of possibilities. Follow your intuition.

Such a ceremony will bring up feelings of sadness of course, and it isn't easy to choose to face those. But it is a beautiful thing to create a sense of respect, honouring that spirit for the time it was with you, and accepting its choice to leave. Maybe even thanking it for the gifts you now see resulted from his or her choice. Some people have found some peace and acceptance of the situation through a process like this.

These are just some of the ways that society can interfere with our ability to process our own death and that of others. We are not supposed to die, death is a failure, death is best outsourced and not mentioned in polite conversation. Hopefully the increased awareness of the effect of unprocessed trauma will help shift this unsupportive attitude a bit closer to what our ancestors knew – and many communities around the world still know. That death is a sacred transition. An illuminated moment in our life journey. We can run from it but then we miss what it can teach us.

> *"There is no such thing as a problem without a gift for you in its hands. You seek problems because you need their gifts." Richard Bach, Illusions: The Adventures of a Reluctant Messiah*

Euthanasia

This is an emerging issue. Although arguably assisted dying has been widespread for centuries through healers and traditional practices – or a gentle nudge from an understanding doctor. However, the increased accountability and safeguarding now in place in many countries have forced this choice to be either legislated or banned.

At the time of writing euthanasia or assisted dying are only available in a handful of countries – though this has been increasing, so may change in the future. Currently the options are Benelux (Belgium, Luxembourg, The Netherlands), Switzerland, Colombia, Canada, New Zealand and Australia (all states but with different criteria), Portugal (awaiting regulation) and Spain. Assisted suicide is allowed in ten of the US states.

There are strict conditions, which may include for example unbearable suffering, the person being of right mind when they

(Elliott)make the decision and a natural death being in the foreseeable future. There is a lively debate about unbearable mental suffering vs physical suffering as it is considered more difficult to evaluate. The evaluation usually must be carried out by at least two independent medical practitioners. In most countries it is also necessary to already be a citizen of that country.

VSED is another option related to euthanasia (Voluntarily Stopping Eating or Drinking). As this will usually take a few weeks from the beginning of the fast to death, the person making this choice will need a lot of physical and emotional support as they weaken. It is not an easy thing for family members who may feel the urge to intervene, offering eg ice chips or tiny amounts of food to alleviate suffering. But although such an offer might seem merciful in the moment, it is likely to prolong the process which could make it even harder for the person who has chosen VSED. There is a lot of information available to make this a better understood concept and process for everyone involved.

> *"Many people struggle with the unrelieved suffering of a chronic or incurable and progressive disorder. Others may decide that they are simply "done" after eight or nine decades of a fully lived life. Free will and the ability to choose are cornerstones of maintaining one's quality of life and dignity in their final days."* (Compassion and Choices, 2022)

Journalist Sophie Mackenzie has written a beautiful article about her own experience of this when her mother made the choice to die this way. See references at the end of the book to read the full story.

> *"Mum was a very private person. She loved order; she hated mess and squalor, and illness is often messy and squalid. She told Vicky again and again that she*

didn't want to go through more treatment. She didn't want Dad to see cancer killing her. She wanted to die quickly and quietly. She didn't want any fuss."

"My sisters Vicky and Jassy and I were with her. We held her hands, told her how much we loved her, and that it was safe and right for her to go. After a few minutes, her breathing stopped. It was a good death – the kind of death I think most people would choose if we could: free from pain and surrounded by love. She wasn't hooked up to tubes or monitors; she was even wearing her own pretty nightdress rather than a hospital gown." (Mackenzie, 2012)

Olivia's story

Olivia has motor-neurone disease. This rare and debilitating condition, also known as ALS, affects the brain and nervous system, decreasing the person's capacity over time to manage their own movements. There is no cure, though there are symptom management treatments that can allow someone with this condition to live for many years. Stephen Hawking managed to continue for 55 years after first developing the disease in his early 20s.

"I think part of his longevity may have been because he had a slowly progressive form. Probably it was also due to the exclusive nursing and medical care that he received." (Elliott) NBC News

However Olivia's condition is advancing more rapidly, and she is likely to be in the more typical category of patients that die within 5 years of developing the disease.

She has done her research and knows that things will just get worse from now on, until her life will end when she can no longer breathe or function. They could of course keep her going for longer if she stays in bed hooked up to life support machines. She shudders at the thought. Never!

Between now and that point she knows she will gradually lose functionality. First becoming clumsier and less able to walk, then struggling to feed herself until eventually she needs everything doing for her.

She cannot believe it.

Until a few months ago Olivia was the founder and CEO of a big social media company. She had ideas, vision, drive! It had broken her heart to have to hand over responsibility for her business years earlier than she'd expected to. But she could feel herself struggling, and the last thing she wanted was for any of her employees to see her as anything other than the tough sharp leader she has always been. So she made her excuses about needing time for a new phase in her life and bowed out. It takes all of her will power not to call the new CEO every day and point out where they are going wrong.

Nobody knows about her condition.

She has always been a fiercely independent woman, loves her spacious apartment with its sweeping views of the city, her nippy red sports car and regular skiing holidays. She worked hard at school and had a relentless work ethic combined with an entrepreneurial streak that had got her to such a good position. But what good was all this success and money to her now? She feels like this cruel twist of fate has cut her off at the knees. She rages every day about her situation.

She still feels she has little in common with her parents and three siblings, who are all still living what she considers to be their very small lives, in the town where they grew up. She feels like they don't really approve of her success, or her life choices, so she has had less and less to do with them over the years. She certainly doesn't feel like crawling back with a serious health condition to deal with their opinions and advice.

And somehow, Olivia was always too busy working and flying around the world to find a husband. She tried the odd bout of internet dating, but it was so time consuming and every man she met seemed to be daunted by her success. After a few attempts she'd give it up as a bad job for another couple of years.

She has friends of course - but they're more the kind of friends for cocktails and a laugh. Humble bragging about their latest business achievements and luxury lifestyle.

Not the kind of friends she would want to see her when she can no longer brush her hair or put on her lipstick. Or show any weakness at all to be honest.

She cannot bear the idea of this undignified decline and slow painful death, dependent on strangers to wash and feed her and using up all her hard-won wealth on personal services. After a few days of analysing the options, she makes her choice. That she will manage her death as competently and efficiently as she has managed her life - and avoid this dreadful decline into dependency.

However there are no euthanasia options available in the UK, where Olivia lives. So she checks herself into the Swiss clinic Dignitas. A not for profit that provides an Assisted Dying service. They have some mixed reviews but overall seem to have the most experience. The cost of $12,000 for the full service (no family involved) seems well worth it for what it will save her in personal compromises.

She writes her will, sorts out her finances and leaves letters to be distributed to her family and the press after she is gone. She empties her fridge and is relieved she never acquired any pets to have to farm out. Lastly, she donates to the Motor Neurone Disease Association.

Because she must travel to Switzerland, she realises she will have to bring the date of her death forward, so she is still fit enough to make the flight alone, sooner than she might prefer. She doesn't want to implicate anybody else given the legal status of her choice and decides against even using an unknown chaperone:

> *"British law states anyone who is said to have encouraged or assisted the suicide or attempted suicide of another person can be jailed for up to 14 years."* (Bird, 2022)

She knows that some people find it hard to go through with the process when it comes to it, but she has always been a determined woman and Olivia implements her decision without a hitch.

This story can raise quite a few questions for our consideration.

How does Olivia's story make you feel? She is quite a particular kind of person. How would her decision-making process have been different if she had a less decisive or rational personality type? How do you think her family members will react when they get the letters and it's too late to do anything? Does she have any responsibility towards them? Maybe you know someone who is considering or has considered this choice. What role could you play to hold integrity and compassion in their presence?

Section 4: Caring for the dying

The importance of not knowing

In my 20s I knew everything. At least I thought I did. I had clear views on human rights, women's rights, the environment – and why so many people were wrong and needed to change.

I had studied mathematics at university and was working in the rational-based world of the oil and gas industry. Yes, despite my environmentalism... I really thought I was going to change their minds and fix things from the inside. It took me 15 years to get over that idea.

Within this well-defined world I was walking through the backstreets to my nearest underground station in North London on my way to work. I saw a strangely dressed middle aged woman up ahead and wondered about crossing the road to avoid her. Something about her movements felt off.

Shrugging off my instincts I carried on. As I neared her the atmosphere thickened with the stench of someone living on the streets. I realised she looked oddly shaped because she was wearing a vast array of clothes. Layer upon layer of torn cardigans, scarves, jackets, more than one hat. My disquiet increased and I was regretting my decision to carry on walking towards her. But it was too late now. It would look far too obvious if I crossed over. English politeness just wouldn't allow it. I held my breath to reduce the smell and continued.

"Help me!" she screeched when I was almost upon her.

I flinched. Looked around. The normally busy streets were suddenly deserted. The traffic had all disappeared. Even the birds seemed to stop singing. It felt like the universe zoomed in on the two of us. That there was nothing else for an instant.

I tried to carry on walking past and a bony hand shot out and grabbed my arm.

"Help me! My heart is on fire!"

Now that got my attention. For a second, I looked at her, then realised I was now involved. I wasn't getting away from this one. But what on earth was I supposed to do?

She let go of my arm and started pulling frantically at her layers of clothes and pointing at the charred clothing.

"Look! It's my heart!"

At first, I assumed she must have got too close to a fire but indeed as she peeled off the clothing, every layer was more burnt than the previous one, the worst being the greying vest next to her skin. It really did look for all the world like her heart had burnt through them.

Now what? I felt compassion for the woman of course. She was genuinely distressed. I had the urge to help her but nothing in my school first aid course had covered what to do in the case of a heart on fire.

I was stumped. Now I truly knew what NOT knowing felt like. I used the only tool in my toolbox at the time and tapped into what my yoga teacher would say. I breathed away my logical analytical mind. Somehow, I realised it was no use to me in this situation. Instead, I breathed into the back of my head, the back of my heart. I needed a bigger solution.

Then, as I looked over my shoulder at the deserted street, hoping I could drag somebody else into the situation, I gasped. At the corner at the top of the road, almost shimmering, appeared an ambulance. It heaved towards us, and I waved frantically. To my relief, it stopped next to us, and a couple of paramedics hopped out.

> "We're not supposed to just stop like a taxi you know! You must call emergency services."

> "I'm sorry," I replied, indicating my companion "But I just don't know what to do."

After examining the woman with the burning heart and realising I had no previous connection to her, they agreed to take her with them and see if someone at the hospital could help.

> "At least they'll get her cleaned up and get some ointment on that burn. Maybe refer her to the psych ward."

A few minutes later they zoomed off and I was alone again in the deserted street. Like it had never happened.

And this, in a way, is how every death feels. However much we know, every death is different. Every human is different. Every family dealing with the death is different. Most of all, every dying person is different. To be truly present we must let go of our thinking, analytical mind and turn instead to our hearts. To *feel* what is needed. To stand in our own humility, our own not knowing and still stay in the situation.

We are never going to be an expert on someone else's death. But we can always be there for them. We can acknowledge them and their grief or fear or anger or acceptance. We can hold space to manifest the support they need. We can surrender into the space behind us and be present in as pure a heart as possible.

We accept that we don't *know* what to do. Focus instead on what we *are*, who the other *is*, and the space between us. Commit to being in that space, to staying fully present, even when that experience is confusing, terrifying, humiliating – or just plain boring.

And, to arm ourselves with more knowledge, more stories, more understanding.

You may even choose to move into the end-of-life business in some format. I was surprised when conducting research with women over 45 without any formal qualifications and currently working in low grade minimum wage jobs. We talked at length about their childhood dreams, their unrecognised skills, their buried yearnings. When we got to discussing specific jobs, across a hundred different women all over the country the most popular idea was to work in a funeral home. They loved the idea of caring for the dead, making things as good as they can be in the circumstances and working in a quiet environment.

This might not be your choice – or mine – but it is a worthy option. There are also possibilities as a humanist funeral celebrant, a member of a Threshold Choir (singing at the deathbed), a grief counsellor, palliative care nurse – or of course my own path, as an End-of-Life doula.

End-of-Life Doulas

The concept of End-of-Life Doulas – those choosing to accompany the dying on their journey, has been around since time began, though mostly lost in the "civilised" modern Western world. However it is a growing area of interest now as more and more individuals wish to have agency in their own death, to choose their place and manner of dying, to define the level of medical intervention they wish for. Even to choose the time and method.

In the UK, the End-of-Life Doulas Association (eol-doula.uk) has a growing membership of professionally trained End-of-Life Doulas working independently with the dying and their families. Recently they have also participated in some government funded programs to provide that same service to those who cannot afford to commission it independently. Pilot programs have been running in Yorkshire (Northern England) and Richmond (near London). A recently commissioned independent report into the efficacy of the program had this to say about an End-of-Life Doula service:

> *"We have noted that this can improve someone's wellbeing – both for the client who is dying but also for those around them – as well as reduce hospital admission...There is an indication that the doula service can support people to live and die well in a manner that is aligned with the local integrated care board's objectives and values." (Prof Erica Borgstrom, 2023)*

Guidelines for caring for the dying

If you have the challenge and the privilege of accompanying someone on their journey towards death, I'd like to mention a few things I believe are worth bearing in mind:

- Your job is to bear witness, not to do or say any "right" thing so let yourself off that idea. Your presence is what matters. The person you are caring for may be a different gender, race, age, sexual orientation, religion – they might be different from you in so many ways. Not to mention the whole of their life experience to date. So don't expect to understand them as well as you will want to. Accept them and be there for them.

- Use your feelings not your head. We have been so filled with strange ideas about death from our upbringing, the media, the world we live in, that it can be easy to get caught in circular thinking and trying to "solve the problem of death". Try to relax into your body, breathe, feel the ground under your feet and listen to your heart. Tread carefully and trust your intuition.

- Be led by what is desired in the heart and soul of the dying person, not what society says 'should' happen. They may have some unusual ideas or some fascinating ones. Encourage them to get past the "but my mother-in-law wouldn't approve ..." statements and closer to their own truth. This is their show.

- Consider yourself first, only then can you help others. This is important work and must be sustainable for us too, especially when death takes much longer to arrive than expected. Take good care of yourself, find someone to talk to, decompress, have rests. There is no amount of effort you can put in that will feel enough, so do what you can with good grace and look for other solutions for the rest. I am often surprised by how happy people are to help, once they know what is expected of them. Taking care of yourself isn't selfish, it's a prerequisite for having strength and love to help others.

- Learn how to say no. This might be on behalf of what you can do yourself – of course you want to do everything you can for the person who is dying, but you may also have your own family, job, health or sanity to take care of. Learn to set boundaries. It may also be on behalf of the dying person. Maybe they really don't want any visitors. Or medication. Or to watch yet another episode of their favourite soap opera. Maybe they just want peace and quiet.

- Just be you. We are so good at seeing how other people do things better than us. That friend who always seems to know the right thing to say, the other one who is so kind and loving. There will always be someone more efficient, more powerful, more gentle, more creative, more patient... we do not have to be any of these people. That is their strength and their contribution to the situation. We are there to show up as ourselves. To be the best version of ourselves for sure. On the days when we can. But sometimes we will be impatient, or thoughtless or irritable. Sometimes we will be tired or hungry or sad or confused. It can help to notice and learn, but not to judge and criticise ourselves for every time we are less than 100% amazing. If we can be gentle and compassionate towards ourselves, then it is easier to be the same towards others.

- Trust yourself. Trust the process. Trust the universe. Trust the other person. Ah yes. Trust. Pick up the average newsreel or conversation at the bus stop and you will likely hear much more about who you shouldn't trust. We are coached in wariness – don't trust strangers / men / foreigners / teenagers / bankers / neighbours. Doubtless a minority of people don't have our best interests at heart, and we should take sensible precautions. But let's not forget the value of trust. Most people do the right thing most of the time. Including ourselves. So I encourage you to trust that your heart already knows what to do. Trust that the person who is dying – including when that is us – will do so in the way that is right for them. Let go of the urge to control and manage this unmanageable process. Breathe.

- Above all, hold compassionate presence. For you. For the person who is dying. For anyone else in the room. For anyone in the world.

Compassionate presence

If you take nothing else from this book, I hope you take this. Compassionate presence is the single most important gift we can give to a dying person. To a living person too.

> *"The highest refinement of love is compassion"*
> Osho, revolutionary mystic.

Compassion contains no quid pro quo. It is much closer to unconditional love, detached love. Not love of an object, or of a person as an object. No sense of possession. No expectations.

Compassion can be defined as a combination of empathy, kindness, concern – and an absence of judgement.

We can feel this pure form of love for someone we have never met. Sometimes more easily than for someone we know only too well! Maybe for you, as for me it feels like a vibration in your body. Like a frequency I tune into when I am fully present. It is still there when words fail us, when we have no idea what to do next, when nothing else will help.

Practice with nature. Trees, rocks, animals. Try stroking them without being present. Just going through the motions. And then again with your full attention, with compassion. They will notice the difference and react in distinct ways. They are showing you they feel it.

Practice with strangers on the bus or in a cafe. You don't even need to look at them (that could get weird). Just tune into them and send them compassion. Sometimes you will see their expression change. A frown might relax, or hunched shoulders drop. They might give a small sigh or a twitch of a smile. Sometimes you see nothing and that's fine too. You're not doing it for your own gratification, no quid pro quo. It's compassion practice. And tuning up your ability to access compassion is reward enough.

Practicing with plants is intriguing. They often start to move, even though there is no breeze. Acknowledging the compassion, sending their own back. They can offer you a shared, nourishing moment in the middle of a tricky day. And demonstrate how offering compassion always gives us personal benefits too. We breathe better, move better, feel more aligned to our own humanity.

Here are seven acknowledged benefits of practicing compassion – quite aside from the benefit for the recipient, these are the ways being compassionate can improve *your* life:

1. **Enhanced emotional well-being**: enjoy the feelgood factor as endorphins spread through your body when you are kind or show empathy to another person.
2. **Reduced stress**: research shows that doing things from compassion for others reduces anxiety because we have moved attention away from ourselves and our own problems.
3. **Increased resilience**: when you practice compassion for others you are also deepening your ability to be compassionate towards yourself. A useful attribute in hard times where you need good coping mechanisms to adapt to challenging circumstances.
4. **Better relationships**: compassion feeds strong relationships. Demonstrating care and understanding for the other person is a tangible way to express love, and empathy makes it easier to see another's point of view and resolve conflicts.
5. **Improved sense of self-worth**: if we see how we are having a positive impact on the lives of others, we know that our lives have meaning and value. We can feel better about ourselves, more confident and with improved self-esteem.
6. **Better physical health**: some of our bodily functions such as immunity and stress related conditions improve when we show compassion towards others.
7. **Other hormonal benefits**: as well as endorphins, mentioned above, our body and sense of well-being benefit from

a. Oxytocin: sometimes known as the love hormone, released for example when we cuddle someone or treat them kindly

b. Serotonin: released by acts of altruism and contributing to a better mood and less depression

c. Dopamine: the reward hormone – this neurotransmitter is released when we do something for another out of compassion. It generates feelings of happiness and satisfaction.

d. Noradrenaline: also released by acts of compassion, it improves alertness and focus which help generate a sense of connection with others

Of course the caveat, as always, is to ensure you also show compassion towards yourself. If your support for another is done from a place of grudging, exhausted or teeth-gritted duty, then you are less likely to get these hormonal rewards. Give yourself time and space to keep good balance between your own needs and the needs of the person you are caring for.

Compassion fatigue is a very real problem that can often affect those caring for the dying – either in a personal capacity or professionally. Know your boundaries, make sure you take time to recharge your own batteries, drop the idea of being perfect or doing everything the person wants of you, forget the idea of "fixing" the dying process.

Don't get to the point of one client a colleague of mine walked in on. She was thumping the wall and screaming at her husband – bed ridden and requiring a lot of care.

"Just bloody well hurry up and die, won't you?"

This is a terribly sad situation for all concerned. The poor woman was at the very end of her resources. Drained to the last drop of energy and compassion. Sometimes we need to be firm with clients about the need for respite care. For everyone's sake.

Be compassionate towards yourself, fill yourself up, then your overflowing compassion can support others too. See the chapter in Section 2 on self-care for more information on this and keep an eye on yourself. Nobody expects you to be a saint or a martyr. Your support is most sustainable when it works for you too.

How does dying look?

There are immense amounts of material available about dying, death, near death, funerals and grief. Extend your research as much as works for you. At the same time, bear in mind that none of these materials are going to solve the problem. There is lots of useful material, and some of it can be a great comfort when you embark on what can feel like a very lonely and unrecognisable journey, but there isn't a death manual that will give you all the answers.

It is my view that we all have a lot to learn from death. It is not only something for us to endure when someone close to us dies. It is also an opportunity to learn, to grow, to develop new skills. It may take a long time to be able to feel that way, when you are in the throes of grief, but it might be worth reflecting on one day.

It can be helpful, as we do on the Sacred Death course, to make a list of all the people we know of who have died. Some will be very close – grandparents for many people, maybe parents or siblings or our own children. Others will be people we knew well – work colleagues, neighbours, friends. And others will be more distant – the baker, a celebrity, someone on the news.

You don't need to create a complete list, but many people come up with 50-100 names quickly.

Reflect on this list. Might some of them be called a "good death"? Why? What constitutes that for you? What about your own role? Maybe you wish you had been there more for the dying person, or have something you'd have liked to say to them before it was too late? Maybe you were able to be fully present – what did you learn from that experience? How has it changed you?

What you are likely to observe is how different each death is. There's the way it happens – home or hospital, expected or a shock, conscious or not, painful or not. And how the person who was dying reacted - if you witnessed that. And probably your own response to the death. How much did it touch you? Deaths we can identify with, even of someone we don't know well, can be more unsettling than a death that feels unlikely to befall us personally. I know that for myself, once I had my first child, I felt very differently about the deaths of either children, or the parents leaving them behind before they were fully grown.

So whatever your experiences, direct or via reading or absorbing other people's stories, I recommend approaching every death with what Zen Buddhists call *beginner's mind*.

> *"In the beginner's mind there are many possibilities,*
> *but in the expert's, there are few." (Suzuki, 1970)*

It is a curious paradox that the more experience we have of something the less likely we are to be open to new information. Keep this concept in mind and allow yourself to be a complete beginner in every situation. Even in every conversation. What you knew yesterday might not be helpful today. How you think the person who is dying will want something, based on a whole lifetime of habits, may change quite suddenly. This might be especially noticeable regarding their views on religion or spirituality. A last-minute urge for reflection or reconnection with an earlier belief system. Or a rejection of something they have appeared to believe for decades. Be ready for anything. Open mind, open heart.

Life expectancy

Nonetheless, it is helpful to have some information about things which could happen during the dying process, so that they don't catch you by surprise if they show up. As I've said earlier, in the west we all tend to have very little contact with death. So things that might be widely known in a society where most deaths take place in the home, have been forgotten in our more medicalised model.

Life expectancy has been generally increasing from 50 years in USA, 48 in Europe in 1900, to much higher now.

There are discrepancies – the world we live in is far from fair. So while we all expect to die one day, there are wide variations. For instance a white woman in the USA can expect an average of 81 years of life, while for a black man it is only 67. And men living in deprived areas in the UK have ten years less life expectancy than their more affluent counterparts. We know the stories, the many adjacent factors of less healthy diet, less likely to be able to take time off sick, more cramped housing, more dampness or vermin. More smoking, less exercise (who can pop off to the gym if they're working three jobs and using every penny to survive?), sometimes less nutritional or healthcare knowledge. Not to mention the much-reported discrepancies in response to patient reported pain:

"Black Americans are systematically undertreated for pain relative to white Americans." (Kelly M. Hoffman, 2016)

That differing response to black people's pain, along with the legacy of zoning laws in the USA means both black mothers and their babies are almost 3 times as likely to die during the birthing process. No wonder the overall life expectancy is different.

A general increase in life expectancy can be seen across the world, at differing speed. In Indonesia for example, the average was only 42 years in 1950 but is 70+ today. Over the same period, life expectancy in Ethiopia has increased from 32 to 68 years.

It is worth noting that although life expectancy has gone up globally (currently an average of 72 years) the likely end of healthy life has not kept pace. We are increasing the amount of time we spend in a state of frailty or reduced capacity.

You may be curious to check out a rough estimate of your probable life span based on a small number of demographic and lifestyle data points. See blueprintincome.com/tools for an example. I'm cheered to see that mine is 94 – but also not surprised as I come from a family of females having long and healthy lives. As DNA profiling increases, we are likely to see more refined prediction tools. An uncomfortable thought if life insurance companies can get their hands on that data.

Regardless of our gender, hometown, race or DNA though, the end will come, sooner or later. And it's not likely to match a website calculation! You will die one day, at least based on current science (Death Deniers perk up... maybe you will have your choice at immortality – whatever that might look like. You can always hope). And even before our own end we are likely to have parents or friends dying, so it helps to know what sort of things can happen.

Death expectancy

The likelihood of seeing friends and relatives who have already passed on, goes up in the last days and hours of a person's life. This phenomenon is widely recognised by medical staff, but not discussed. As covered in respected neuroscientist Marjorie Hines Wollacott's book "Infinite Awareness" (Woollacott, 2015) this places the phenomenon in the category of 'anecdotal research' which tends to be disregarded by medical science. A similar problem arises with NDEs (near death experiences). Although she details, in her book, some staggeringly precise evidence of out-of-body observations during "brain dead" episodes, she also explains that since it is not possible to do a double-blind experiment it cannot be taken as scientific fact.

However research in this area is increasing and hopefully it will reach a level of legitimacy where relatives are not alarmed by their dying family member talking to a departed relative as though they were in the room with them. Which to the minds of the family cannot be true since they cannot see or hear a dead person.

> *Visions and vivid dreams are end-of-life experiences that are seldom talked about. They often include reunions with deceased loved ones — and can provide dying patients with profound comfort. (Orlando, 2021)*

This article quotes Christopher Kerr, now CEO of Hospice & Palliative Care Buffalo and author of Death is but a Dream, based on 1400 interviews with dying patients under strict research conditions. He considers the point of view that although the physical body is in a state of decline as death approaches, the spiritual being within each person is in a state of rapid growth and transformation. In part this spiritual awakening manifests as visions or vivid daydreams, often involving friends and relatives that have already died.

> ... And the end story is that nearly 90 percent of people, within the days and weeks before death, have at least one of these events that are defined by being extraordinarily real and profoundly meaningful. They increase in frequency as people get nearer to death. (Kerr, 2020)

So these two aspects of dying are important for all of us to acknowledge. Firstly that we may have interactions with what might be considered ghosts (fear of these beings by the dying person is unusual, they are much more likely to bring comfort) and secondly that someone may choose to die in a moment when alone, rather than surrounded by friends or relatives.

In the Discover article, Kerr goes on to comment on an important aspect of reclaiming death:

> "Dying is inherently isolating. And we've dehumanized it in so many ways. Yet this serves as one mechanism by which we can humanize what is a very human experience. What this research does, I hope, is take dying from being viewed as organ failure to the closing of a life.

> We are so much more than failing parts.

> I think what's important, on the caregiving side, is giving hospice patients the permission for these experiences to be expressed. And the bereaved are

typically a part of that story, so it feels like people are brought together."

It would also help to give medical staff more freedom to acknowledge these likely events to friends and family visiting the dying.

Another aspect of dying of which it is useful to be aware, is terminal restlessness or agitation. During this phase of the dying process the individual may pluck at bedclothes, fidget, pick at scabs, pace about if they are able and generally find it hard to settle.

This can be hard to observe as caregivers try their best to calm the person and give them some peace. It may be caused by physical factors relating to the cause of death eg changes in hydration, organ function, pain management, medications or disrupted sleep patterns. There may also be emotional factors such as fear of death, unfinished business or concern about arrangements following their death. Sometimes there may be guilt or a sense of failure, that one's life wasn't good enough. Or fear of retribution – awaiting punishment.

I have had patients admit past acts which they have kept secret and felt bad about, sometimes for decades. They are looking for forgiveness and while some may get that from their religion – such as the absolution of sins part of the Catholic ceremony of Last Rites – I personally feel that we are all entitled to forgiveness and can all offer this to each other.

Distress at the thought of dying and fear of what comes next for the person facing that journey is also not easy to witness. Our urge to care for and fix each other might hit a brick wall. Who are we to say everything will be fine when the dying person is about to undergo something of which we have no personal experience?

And yet comfort and reassurance may be the best we can offer. Back to compassionate presence. Witnessing their suffering. Not plastering over it or telling them to stop feeling that way, but staying present, holding space for them to feel their feelings and express them if they wish to.

Having said all this, a troubled death is not the norm for many people.

> *Professor Dame Lesley Fallowfield professor of psycho-oncology at the University of Sussex, commented that "normal" deaths are rarely depicted in popular culture, but that "for many individuals, death is a gentle, peaceful and pain-free event."*
>
> *(Gander, 2019)*

If a peaceful death is our aim, then there are ways to improve our chances.

One is to plan ahead (see later Section 7 about End-of-Life Planning). As much as possible aim for your death to happen in the way you wish it too. In the place where you want to be, with the people you want to have with you.

This is a time you can indulge yourself. What will make you more comfortable? Smooth sheets? A soft pillow? A perfect cup of tea in your favourite mug? Music can be a great source of comfort and it can be worth thinking about playlists in advance to help anyone caring for you to know they are giving you exactly what you want.

There are plenty of ideas in the Section 7. But a good start is to imagine your perfect day then zoom in on the details that make it just what you want.

As well as the dying process, there are things that can be done at any point in our lives up until that moment. Cleaning up as we go with our relationships can increase our general peace of mind and leave less room for last minute regrets. On a practical level too, getting rid of unwanted possessions and tidying up your finances might enhance your life while you are still living, as well as bringing more ease to your death – and reducing the aftermath for those who will have to deal with it.

Some of the physical signs of death drawing near include a waxy pallor or mottling on the skin, cold hands and feet, loss of appetite, sleeping a lot of the time and dry mouth. Vital signs (eg blood pressure, heart rate) may decrease, and breathing will become slower and shallower, possibly laboured. Urination can decrease too along with the dying person having a general lack of interest in anything going on around them. It's best too of you can avoid hoping for some brilliant insights or life changing words as someone dies. That's common in the movies and soap operas, much less so in real life. They may say something inaudible, or mundane or nothing at all. Your job is to let them go anyway.

Every death is different

Here are a few stories based on people I have met or worked with. Again I have changed the names and some personal details to protect the privacy of those involved. Sometimes it can be easier to consider these issues at the arms-length of being a third party, rather than to think of someone we are close to. I know that every person I work with is also a teacher for me. Are there any learnings you can find for yourself here?

I invite you to feel into each of these personalities and their circumstances to see what resonates, or what is triggered, for you.

Liz's story: fearing death

Liz is a white woman in her late 60s who has terminal cancer. It is one year since her diagnosis, when she was told she had maybe as few as four months, or as many as 18, to live. You will have encountered your own death stories as well, I'm sure. Maybe what is different is you can consider these examples in a more objective way.

Emotional / psychological situation

She is generally a nervous and unconfident person, especially in groups. Medical staff describe her as "needy". She is fearful about death and struggles to accept the idea that it will happen to her soon. Even though she is very negative about her life she is still afraid to face death, partly because of shame she feels about her life.

She has experienced death by cancer first-hand when she nursed her husband through cancer until he died two years ago.

Her son shares her passions for art history and architecture. He lives two hours away though, with his wife (who Liz believes doesn't like her) and teenage children, so is "too busy" to visit. She is not part of a church or spiritual community and doesn't know her neighbours very well, so feels quite isolated. She doesn't feel like there is anyone she can call on for help.

She is an alcoholic and has used drugs, but she went through the AA 12 steps program and has been clean and sober for a few years. It is still part of her identity though, and one of the ways she berates herself.

Physical situation

She is frustrated by her physical weakness and the huge effort it takes to move. She can still walk but barely does. Just taking a few steps exhausts her. She feels a lot of pain in her feet and ankles from swelling.

She lives alone, likes her garden – though is frustrated by how much of a mess it looks, now she can no longer look after it. She has a whole room devoted to craft making but feels she can no longer do any of it – although she did get involved with some activities at one of her respite visits to the hospice which suggested she could do still something if she allowed herself to lower her standards. She is still interested in books about art and art history.

Considering this limited information about Liz, have a think about how you might help make things easier for her, if you had responsibility for that. What could you change or arrange? What more might you need to know? How would you deal with the fact that she is well practiced at pushing people away while resenting them for leaving? Does this situation remind you of anything in your own life?

Abdul's story: slow decline

Abdul is a very tall young man in his mid 20s with a muscular wasting disease. None of the staff at the hospice knew him earlier in his life, so their only experience of him is in the current advanced state of his disease. He is thought to be within a few months of the end of his life.

He is in a specially built wheelchair which allows him to lie almost flat at night to sleep, as he can't be easily moved by his parents who take care of him. He spends all his time in this wheelchair except for bathing, once a week, when he comes to the hospice where they have hoist facilities in the bathroom.

He is near the end of his illness and now cannot move much at all, though he can sometimes manage a thumbs up to show his agreement with a suggestion.

He is usually calm and seems to be accepting of both his disease and his premature death.

Nobody knows his spiritual beliefs, especially since he was a child when he first started to be affected, and the chances are that like many young people, he has revised his views from the way he was brought up. As he can no longer speak it would take a lot of patient enquiry to find out.

He can still swallow so is spoon-fed regular food that has been put through the blender, so he doesn't need to chew it. He is clear about what foods he likes and doesn't like so staff feel they can give him his favourites.

He is very popular with the hospice staff who like to flirt with him. They were extremely kind and friendly towards him, but I felt that, maybe had lost sight of the young man inside. It is so easy to slip into a patronising relationship with those in advanced stages of disease or dying. All jolly and smiley but not working as equals. It's a safe place to operate from. It is uncomfortable to be confronted with suffering and mortality, our ego wants to run from it, so it looks for ways to avoid the problem. It's natural and nothing to be ashamed of. It is though, something to be aware of, so we can decide if this is really the way we want to be.

As a volunteer in these situations, I was able to observe both my own reactions – some more helpful than others – and those of other people. I saw how visitors to the hospice might completely avoid the topic of the person dying, chattering away instead about their everyday lives in a wall of sound that left no gaps for emotional disclosure. Small wonder that cliches are resorted to so often. Really saying what we feel may seem unimaginable. And depending on the person who is dying, disclosure could go against their culture and upbringing, causing more awkwardness, than if the elephant in the room were left to sleep peacefully in the corner.

Others use humour as a shield.

> "Don't worry, Bob, we'll break you out of here in a couple of days then we can all go down the boozer!"

> "Steady on old girl, we can't have you running off with the handsome doctor now, can we?"

It may help get through an awkward moment – or it may only help the person who is saying these things, leaving the dying patient feeling even worse. Sometimes when these visitors leave, I have seen patients slump back, exhausted from the effort of keeping up pretences for 45 minutes.

The atmosphere in a hospice or medical facility can become very specific. Those arriving from the outside world can be a welcome breath of fresh air, or their presence can jar, feeling too loud, too insistent and out of synch with the feelings inside the place they are visiting.

There is no right and wrong. Though there's a place for heartfelt stance of curiosity about the dying person's state of mind and heart that day, and there may well be a place for a distractingly amusing anecdote. There are no hard and fast answers here, just a suggestion that we tune in. It's ok to say nothing for a minute while you align with the person you are visiting, and the place they are in. Try matching their breathing rhythm. Or mirroring their posture if they are sitting up. These small shifts in our consciousness help position us in the room and in the shoes – or bed - of the dying person.

Physical mirroring in whatever way we can is a good way to start to bridge the gap between our world and that of the people we are supporting. Squatting by a wheelchair instead of booming down at someone, letting ourselves be still instead of rushing around. Try eating with a knife and fork wearing thick gloves to have some empathy with someone whose motor skills feel like that. Luckily, we get a taste of this whenever we are ill or injured ourselves. Tap back into your muscle memory from those experiences and see how it also altered your outlook, your behaviour, your ability to respond.

I was shocked when, during project work in a Syrian refugee camp, I had to change into the same clothes as the local women and immediately felt physically and emotionally different. I hadn't worn a long tunic like that before, especially a thick heavy scratchy one. I felt so restricted. I couldn't lift my arms above my shoulders because of the cut and the heaviness weighed on my chest. When I started to walk, I noticed the stiff fabric stuck out in front so I couldn't see the rough, uneven ground of the camp. I immediately felt smaller, less powerful, hesitant. I hadn't expected that. Of course, the clothing was more of a shock for me than for someone who had grown up wearing it, but even so it was fascinating to see how it changed me. At the end of the day when I could take it off, I danced around the room filled with a sense of freedom. I'd seen the same in the women in the camp when I ran a dance club session for them and blacked out the windows.

Nobody can easily "take off" a terminal health condition and dance around the room. But for those of us walking alongside them on their journey we might find it useful to feel a little bit of their lived reality.

It might feel easier then, with that experience, or even just that mindset, to pitch your interactions. In fact, it's perfectly ok to say nothing the whole time you are visiting. You might just hold their hand or be in peace at their side. In companiable silence. It doesn't come easy, because we are used to a busy life full of noise, but it might be just what is needed on that occasion, by that person.

On this specific day with Abdul, the staff had asked me to wheel him to a separate room to have some time alone after lunch, handing me a soothing CD of meditation music to put on the sound system for him.

He reminded me of a film I had seen "The Fundamentals of Caring" about a young man with a similar condition, though less mild temperament!

In a balanced review of the film, Dominic Evans had this to say:

> "What *Fundamentals* gets right is how some with DMD [Duchenne Muscular Dystrophy] see themselves. My best friend had Duchenne. I have a similar neuromuscular disability. I've been around people with DMD for decades. Many boys/young men are sheltered by their families, especially their mothers. Because many with DMD die between their

late teens and late 20s, most do not go to college, look
for employment, or have Intimate relationships. Some
are led to believe they are just waiting to die." (Evans,
2016)

So back to Abdul. Meditation music just didn't feel quite right so
on a hunch I scanned the box of CDs for sale in the fundraising
room and came back with more options. This was a day when the
thumbs up was hard for him, so I suggested he blink twice for yes
when I showed him the CD he wanted.

When I held up the one from a heavy rock band, I got a clear yes.
Even though I had been told he hadn't been able to move his feet
for months, he was soon tapping his foot to the pounding rhythm
and almost smiling. Well worth the ticking off I got from the area
manager for disturbing the peace!

It was a good reminder for me to always try to see the person
behind the disease. And got me thinking – this young man may
never have been kissed. Or had any sexual experiences. But his
disease wouldn't affect any of those natural urges. I didn't do
anything about that for him, but it would be worth considering if
you are caring for someone who develops a long-term
degenerative condition as a child and may be considered a child
for their whole life because of that. Did anyone ask them about
their bucket list? Are they being allowed some adulthood before
they die?

Rani's story: split loyalties

Rani's children are now adults living in Hong Kong, Singapore,
London and New York. She started to show signs of early onset
dementia at about 50 years old and, after struggling first to
recognise her condition, and then to cope with developing

symptoms, she soon had to give up her job as headteacher of a successful high school.

She was physically well at the time but over the last 8 years has been deteriorating and now lives in a care home about 2 miles from her husband. He visits regularly and does his best to make sure she is well cared for, but he also has a new relationship which his children know about, and struggle with, but he hasn't mentioned to his wife.

It makes for some family tension.

Rani is frightened by her condition and mostly no longer opens her eyes. She spends most of her time in bed and the only nourishment she still has are protein shakes sipped through a straw while someone else holds them. She is expected, by staff at the care home, to die within the next 6-12 months.

Her daughter Rachel lives about two hours train ride away but visits regularly. At first all she could do was sob, flooded with her own grief at seeing her mother "dissolving before my eyes". They had always been very close, and her daughter felt that she was losing her best friend as well as her parent.

Rachel also hated the way her father was testing her loyalty to him with his new relationship and was especially resentful that he was spending family money (so partly her mother's) helping his new girlfriend with unexpected expenses for her and her two children.

Rachel threw herself into her relationship with her mother but was unsure what to do during their time together. This is a common situation and we discussed options such as putting together an album of family holiday snaps or special occasions on her I-pad that they could look through together, giving Rachel a focus and something to talk about in their one-sided conversations.

Sometimes Rani would react to a photo and Rachel felt that they were connecting like before.

Rani's daughter also put together playlists of songs she knew her mother would enjoy. Rani had been a big Abba fan and the catchy tunes seemed to lighten the atmosphere a little in the small room. Another suggestion which Rachel found helpful was to go with a friend. They could talk to each other across the bed about all sorts of things and Rachel could be more relaxed while feeling her mother also in the room. It felt more natural than Rachel doing all the talking on her own, hoping for a response from her mother.

A lovely idea of Rachel's was to take her mum's favourite perfume and spray it on the pillow. Then she would lie next to her, holding her close. Sometimes she felt like her mother was holding her too.

Things get more complicated when Rachel is offered her dream job in San Francisco. She'd been ready to leave her current position for a while, and this is a great opportunity.

She is excited about the job offer but feels terrible leaving her mother. Even though by her own admission her mother scarcely seems to know she is there by then.

She is also worried about leaving her mother in the hands of her father and brothers. Rani's husband and 2 sons take a much more pragmatic approach to her situation – at least that's all they'll admit to. They consider their mother is "basically gone" already so visiting her is not very useful. They also think it is not necessary to have a funeral when she dies, instead suggesting a simple cremation with only immediate family present, then no memorial or gravestone. Rachel wants to celebrate her mother's life and many attributes and achievements. She really wants the clear marker of a funeral full of friends and family sharing stories and appreciating

Rani. Rachel also wants to have a gravestone, even if Rani is cremated, so she always has a place she can go and "be with" her mother.

If you work with the dying you may find yourself in the middle of these differing points of view and split loyalties. We are not here to judge who is right or wrong in this story, but to realise that between them, they are not finding answers acceptable to everyone. Until they are prepared to talk together, giving all members of the family a voice, it will be hard to find some common ground.

It feels more difficult for Rachel because once again she seems to be the odd one out. With her mother in her current condition, Rachel feels like the only female voice in the conversation, as well as being youngest and known within the family as "the sensitive one". She is very conscious of the males all holding one point of view while she has another. They have all left it too late to ask Rani what she wants.

In the end Rachel came to see that her own challenges in life and the therapy and personal development journey she had already taken, might make her the new natural family leader when it came to emotional intelligence. Maybe rather than being at the bottom of the pile she could help support her male relatives in this situation. Maybe of all of them, she was best placed to broach these difficult topics and hold space for the confusing array of feelings that can come up. Once she changed her thinking from being upset with their difficult behaviour, to understanding she might have tools to process emotions and be responsible for guiding them all through these difficult conversations, she found the courage to take action and they all moved forward together to a process that worked for everybody.

André's story: different belief systems

André was a meditation teacher in his mid 30s living for the last six years in a small community in Thailand. His parents and 2 brothers live in France. These events took place during 2020 in the beginnings of the COVID-19 pandemic.

He had recently broken up with his girlfriend and was frustrated by the ongoing affect COVID was having on his work – most of his students had left the island and he had to cancel his retreats. He was short of income but did not feel comfortable about the idea of teaching online.

Recently he had contracted dengue fever and, although physically recovered, still feels mentally very down as his immune system struggles to rebuild after the illness. As noted in an article published in the Indian Journal of Psychological Medicine,

> *"Depression and anxiety are noted to be prevalent during both the acute and convalescent stages of the [dengue] infection" (Damodharan Dinakaran, 2021)*

They talk of figures as high as 60-90% suffering from anxiety and/or depression during the illness and subsequent convalescence with a minority having prolonged or more severe consequences. However, they also point out that the psychological and neurological impact of the viral infection is not well researched, understood or treated.

The combination of heartbreak, illness, financial challenges and possibly dengue related depression were too much for André and he decided to end his own life.

He was discovered a few hours afterwards when resuscitation was no longer an option.

His family were devastated but unable to travel because of COVID restrictions. It would have been very expensive and difficult for them to send the body back to France, especially during COVID.

The family were strongly Catholic, but their son was not, preferring a more spiritual or new age approach. His mother felt the need to give her son a "good Catholic burial" but was not sure whether that is possible as she had heard that suicide is considered murder – indeed the Catechism states,

> "Suicide contradicts the natural inclination of the
> human being to preserve and perpetuate their life."

and therefore maybe he was not allowed to have a Catholic funeral. Maybe, as she has heard some say, he is already in hell. Indeed until 1980 she would have been correct as until then, a Catholic who had died by suicide would not be permitted a funeral mass, or to be buried in a Catholic graveyard.

Luckily these assessments are now more nuanced, often allowing a benefit of the doubt view that the psychological state of someone who feels that taking their own life is the best option in the circumstances, means that they did not take the decision in a state of full free will. You may not agree with this view either, suggesting, as it does, that suicide is only acceptable in a state of diminished responsibility. However it gave André's mother some comfort.

Although Eastern attitudes tend to be more tolerant of suicide, certainly in certain situations (think of the Japanese act of *hara-kiri* were choosing to die slowly and painfully goes some way to mitigate shame or widows in India sometimes throwing themselves onto the funeral pyre of their husband), the general view in Thailand is that suicide is a sin or at the very least foolish act. The local staff where he was staying gave the whole situation a wide berth.

Nobody knew what to do about the funeral and the only person on the ground who is around to make arrangements is André's ex-girlfriend.

Considering this situation, how might you support the family? What do you think they need to hear, so they feel that André's body and soul have been handled well, that he has been shown kindness and compassion? How would you comfort a family who have not only lost a son but cannot attend his funeral?

After Death

We have looked at our existing beliefs and emotions around death, as well as those encouraged in us by the societies in which we live. We have also looked at how we might support those who are dying and how different that can be in every single case. Death is not a standard procedure.

Inevitably we come to the issue of "and then what?" One of the questions I most often get asked as a death doula is:

> "What happens after we die?".

Of course I do not have a special inside track to that information. I don't know the answer to this, any more than anybody else. I have my own views for sure, but it is not my place to share those unless asked. And my views are based on my feelings, everything I've read, who I am, how I respond to difficulties, my degree of optimism – many factors.

So many cultures have strong beliefs in a life after death and believe they have spiritual contact with ancestors that it seems like there is something there. Not something that science can prove - or disprove. One of life's mysteries. Maybe The Life Mystery.

One thing I would urge everyone to do though, when they encounter someone's death, is to take their time. When the person you are with, or connected to in some way, passes away there is rarely a need to leap into action. You will need to call a doctor to verify the death – or in some countries the police – but that can wait a few minutes.

This initial moment of passing is a sacred one, whatever your belief system. It is the final breath of that version of that soul, if you feel they are going on to other forms of existence. Or it is the final breath of that person if you feel this life is it. Either way it is a momentous occasion and one that deserves to be treated with respect and full attention.

Different cultures with spiritual beliefs have differing views about the amount of time it takes a spirit to leave the body; from the Muslim view that the spirit departs immediately, to others stating a specific number of hours or days. My own feeling, as discussed further in Section 8, my shamanic experiences, is that the spirit takes any amount of time to leave – sometimes even years – but this is not always about the human body the spirit had been inhabiting. It might be to do with the place where they died, other people that are being left behind, or any manner of unfinished business.

Whatever your belief system though, death is a moment of change for everyone involved. Taking time to acknowledge that, sit with it, feel into it, may feel better, both in the moment and in retrospect, than rushing into efficient operational mode, unless there is a suspicion of criminal behaviour, and the police need to be informed urgently.

The rules vary country to country, so check if there are any requirements where you are. For example, in England, so long as the death is registered within 5 days, you can keep the deceased person at home.

You might want to spend some time talking to the person who has just died, sharing your feelings, maybe saying anything you wish you had said while they were still there. You might want to sing to them, read to them, lie by their side and hold their hand. Tune in and trust your instincts. This moment, where you start your journey of coming to terms with this person's death, is precious and individual to you. There isn't a right or wrong way to approach it, though I urge being as fully present as you can manage.

Later you may want to arrange the bedclothes, brush their hair, and tend to them as you would if they were alive. If you want to keep eg their wedding ring, then it can be a good idea to remove it straightaway before the body starts to respond to its new state.

Washing the body can be a beautiful way to care for someone dear to you who has passed on. It may feel strange at first, and it might help to have a friend or doula with you. It can feel very calming at this profound moment. Most people find that they warm to the idea and find it soothing and a gratifying way to give service and have a final connection with the person who has died. Even if you don't feel like a full body wash, you could do your own version of this. Maybe sponging down their face, shaving them, hands and feet, rubbing their favourite lotion into their skin, spraying their favourite perfume onto their clothes. These simple quiet moments together can be very precious.

You may also want to dress them in the clothes you feel they would choose, wash and blow dry their hair, do their makeup and manicure if that is what they would have liked. A Funeral Home will of course make the body look as good as they can if you will be having any viewing of the person who has died, but they are unlikely to know your friend or family member they way you did, and I've heard people say they barely recognised their relative after the professional's makeover.

Maybe it feels more appropriate to you to add a dab of your mum's favourite lipstick, those earrings she saved for special occasions and dress her in her smart dress, whether or not anybody else will see her. Or straighten your dad's tie, make sure he is clean shaven, and brylcreem back his hair just the way he'd do it himself. It's a way of saying goodbye.

Many more progressive funeral directors, like Poppy's in the UK can support you if you wish for a more individual response to the death and funeral arrangements. Try searching for "alternative funeral directors" in your area if you feel the traditional approach is not for you.

Death traditions around the world

One of the fascinating exercises on the Sacred Death course is when each participant researches the death traditions of a particular culture or religion and then shares what they have learnt with the group. Hearing the different perspectives shows not only obvious differences that we are already aware of between the major religions but also approaches by specific ethnic groups in the Arctic Circle or the Sahara Desert. It is a rich and fascinating study.

Did you know for instance about the tribe in Toraja, part of Sulewesi in Indonesia, who celebrate each year with their dead family members? Based on a belief that it is important to care for the ancestors, bodies are mummified and return to the family once a year for a change of clothes, maybe a cigarette or a chance to meet new family members.

It seems extraordinary at first, maybe even macabre to our western mindset, but if you look at Claudio Seber's beautiful photos of the get-togethers (Seber, 2017), they seem full of warmth, humour, and the joy of family.

The villagers feel it also makes grieving easier and it makes sense, having cared for family during their lifetime, to keep caring for them.

> "My mother died suddenly, so we aren't ready yet to let her go," a Torajan woman, Yohana Palangda, told National Geographic.

There could be a whole separate book of ideas such as this, which challenge our conventions and may bring us to a more open-minded view of what death is and how we can relate to it. Part of reclaiming death, decolonising death, is breaking away from the idea that what we have been told by the establishment since the Age of Reason, is always right. Opening space for our instincts and intuition and imagination to create ceremonies for our dying and our dead that honour them in ways that make sense to us, even if the result doesn't qualify as what standard Western society would say is a "good funeral".

And while considering this aspect of personal choice, let us hold space for all those peoples around the world who were told by colonisers that their approach of caring for the dying and dead was wrong. Those who were forced to abandon sacred rituals which had brought some sense of peace to the bereaved for hundreds of years, because it became too risky to maintain them. This cultural imposition must have caused many families to feel they were not giving their departed relatives what they needed. A compounding factor to their grief.

I learned from some of the Indonesians and other nationalities attending my Sacred Death training course, that there are challenges with every approach to death. The deep acceptance of dying as a means of moving on, levelling up, becoming an influential ancestor, leaves little room for grief and sadness around death. Or for the dying person to express any fears or regrets about their impending change of status.

Everybody, everywhere, deserves to die and say farewell and grieve in ways that make sense to them. Not to automatically accept the ways that have been sold to us by our culture or religion or local history. We can take solace from well-worn rituals of course, and an element of ritual – wherever it comes from – is valuable to all of us in our processing of our own dying or of others' deaths. I hope that increasingly we develop the capacity to allow ourselves and others to be free to die and grieve in our own way.

Section 5: Secrets, lies and family dynamics

Ah families. What a great source of delight, tension, love, pain and general confusion. All of which can be concentrated around the death bed.

If you are in the position of an End-of-Life Doula or other professional, as an objective, neutral party during someone's death, you will likely have a very different view to those that are embroiled in the years of slights, resentments, triumphs, suspicions, rivalries, love matches and so on that make up the rich, dense patchwork of most families. You may be working with a family who are so tight lipped they can't express their feelings at all. Though of course those feelings will still be in the room, causing situations, even when they are not expressed. Other families will be expressing frequently and strongly – a different dynamic to manage.

I have seen this play out in several ways, all of these are good to be aware of, as you are likely to be a witness to and maybe drawn into the drama. It is always helpful to remember you don't have the answers, it's not your job to fix the problem and, most likely, you don't know the half of it. However, you can suspend judgment and hold compassionate presence for all those involved. Sometimes just allowing people to share their feelings and fears can help untangle these situations. Sometimes the dying person will find the courage to speak their mind and shake things up after a lifetime of keeping quiet.

Old feuds

All families have their histories. And sometimes incidents have been buried, to keep the peace. Under the strain of impending or recent death, those tensions may resurface, possibly in a more dramatic form than originally if feelings have been repressed, or situations resented, for a long time.

It is up to you how much you get involved, but tread carefully. Trying to pull focus back to the dying person and making sure they are centre stage may be helpful. Family difficulties may well need to be processed and dealt with – and sometimes the deathbed is maybe not the time or place. On the other hand, it may be the only time and place where it could ever happen and could be the parting gift of the person who is dying, to have triggered this moment of raw emotion.

Differences of opinion

A key area of potential tension is when different members of the family have different ideas about what the dying person wants and needs. For example a sister may have strong religious views and be convinced that this is what the dying person would want, while the spouse feels they know it certainly isn't.

There can also be differences in views regarding medical treatment.

All of these are helped by listening to the dying person with an open heart and open mind or having a clear End-of-Life Plan. But neither of these options may be available. In this case, the listening must be directed towards the family members with different opinions, trying to get to the bottom of their own hopes and fears that are driving these views. As an objective outsider, you may be able to provide that mediation role and hopefully find ways forward that everyone can be comfortable with.

Secrets and confessions

It is not unusual for someone approaching death to want to wipe the slate clean. Many of us are carrying secrets and cover-ups - sometimes for a very long time.

Some of the things people carry with them and feel bad about may seem very trivial now, in the context of their whole life. But listen with an open heart to whatever they want to share or need to get off their chest.

In my experience, this may include pregnancies nobody ever knew about, extra-marital affairs or other sexual adventures, financial misdeeds, criminal activity, cheating in all kinds of ways or just a long-standing habit of say being nasty to their sister.

I am not an ordained priest or religious representative of any authority, but I feel it is valid in these situations to say "you are forgiven" if that is what the person is seeking. In these last days and hours, forgiveness can bring a profound sense of peace which may be essential for their smooth passing.

Missing persons

It can often be the case that the people who would be there, in an ideal world, are not. Families disperse these days – in many parts of the world we no longer spend our lives near our families of origin. When my grandmother died in England, I was in Colombia with one of her great grandchildren, all her sons were also living overseas, and her husband had died many years earlier. Because the death was unexpected and fast, only her eldest daughter could be at her side.

Some people will tolerate this with great pragmatism, for others it could be a much heavier burden. In modern times we do at least have options like video calls so people can be present to some extent. If you end up in this situation, it can help to have the screen you are talking to at the same kind of place and size as the person would be, it convinces our brain a little more. If you have Bluetooth headphones too, then it feels freer. Before the call, put your attention first on yourself, as we did at the beginning of this book, then on the space and thirdly on the other person. Try and hold the view that it is your presence, your compassionate presence, that is of value, over and above any words you can conjure up.

The COVID 19 pandemic saw an extreme case of this situation, and many felt the compounded grief of losing someone close to them while not being able to hold their hand or care for them. Sometimes we cannot be there when we want to be, or in the way we want to be. Even if you are there, seeing your life partner on the other side of the window covered in tubes and medical staff as they take their last breath or watching them in a coma on life support are also versions of being forced to hold distance. In these situations we need to find other ways to connect with the energy field of the person who is dying. Holding them in our thoughts, in our hearts, speaking to them on an energetic plane when we cannot do so on a conventional one.

In other situations, people may be intentionally absent because of family feuds. I worked with one woman who had left home 30 years earlier after a huge row with her father – sparked by strong differences of opinion about how she should live her life. She had been living in another country for several years when she heard he had died – but was not yet ready to accept their differences and attend his funeral.

When I spoke with her, this was deeply buried, and only brought out into the open because of the experience of sitting with her best friend who was dying. We discussed how it is never too late to put things right. She could still travel in her heart to her father and be open to his death and how it might affect her.

When I saw her the next day, she explained she had spent the whole evening sobbing. Years of bottled-up grief had flooded her system. She realised how this pain had impacted on many of her life decisions. This kind of release can make the intervening years seem like a terrible waste – but this woman would likely live a few more decades herself and both she and her daughter felt it was a significant step forward that would bring them both benefits.

Living with regret is exhausting. On my Sacred Death: Reclaim Dying, Embrace Living course we go through an exercise of each imagining a person whose death was unresolved at the time, lying in front of us. Participants then talk to their person, listen to them, make peace with the moment. It can be very therapeutic.

Alternatively you might be the kind of person who would feel better writing a letter to someone who has departed, saying all the things that were hard to express at the time.

Ongoing resentments

Grief is one of life's great challenges, yet it is beautiful to see how families can pull together to support each other through this journey.

This might not always be the case though. Someone might feel that another family member contributed to the death in some way. Or that a doctor failed them. There is often anger and physical fights can even break out. If someone can hold space for this emotion – not denying or suppressing it but allowing it to flow through instead of getting stuck, then it is less likely to cause long term harm.

Maybe some of these feelings and resentments need to be voiced in the heat of the moment so they can be processed. Grief is an acceptable reason for a lot of behaviour that would otherwise raise eyebrows so maybe this crucible of intense emotion can serve a long-term purpose in a family which doesn't find it easy to share feelings together. Let's look at it in more detail in the next section.

Section 6: Good Grief

Causes of grief

Grief affects us so many times during our lives.

The pioneering midwife Robin Lim, based in Bali and acknowledged by CNN with their hero of the year award in 2011, speaks passionately of our first experience of grief (Lim, 2016). She describes how when we are born and our umbilical cord is cut, separating us from the placenta – seen as the twin in Balinese culture – and from our mother. The new-born baby may be confused by these events, or grief stricken. Lim believes that the more gently the placenta is handled, the better for baby, mother and community.

Sadly in what leading obstetrician Dr Michael Odent refers to as the "industrialisation of childbirth" – also described as the colonisation of childbirth - many placentas are treated as biowaste and discarded with little care – or, when pregnant women have completed a donor form (maybe without appreciating what it means) used for their stem cells and cosmetic research. By contrast, in Bali the placenta is given a ceremonial burial, and every person knows where their placenta, or *birth twin* is buried. I was unaware of this tradition when my own children were born so I'm grateful that my amazing midwife, Becky Reed, encouraged me to look at the placenta each time, and see its beauty, then plant it in my garden – or hers when I lived in an apartment without a garden – with a new tree which could feed from all of that goodness and life force.

As well as this early life event, and the obvious cause of grief – losing someone we care about – most of us experience many types of grief during our lives. We may feel grief for personal events such as the end of a relationship, the end of childhood, leaving a place or country we have lived in, the end of a job, or a career, a dream, our health and mobility, our eyesight, our freedom… the list goes on. And for societal events – the end of a term of office of a leader we admire, the end of freedom for a group of people, the end of the right to abortion or gender fluidity or being able to walk home safely at night.

When somebody loses a person close to them, the grief can be at multiple levels. There is the loss of the person in the first instance, but there may also be loss of lifestyle – if the person who died was the main provider for example – or loss of freedom, if for example, they were the primary carer for the bereaved who may now have to leave their home and go to live in a care facility. There is grief for all that could have been – the planned holidays, the "one day we'll…" dreams. There may be practicalities if the person who died was the only driver, or the one who dealt with all the financial management or did all the cooking. Often couples share tasks between them and whichever one dies that leaves gaps.

These days, many young people suffer from ecological grief – a heightened awareness of the dire position of the planet with respect to climate change and resource management. Unlike their parents and grandparents, many born in the last thirty years have been acutely aware of the climate crisis and the likely impact on their future for their whole lives. They are also more likely to feel the consequences than the preceding generations. This may cause resentment of the baby boomers who caused many of the problems, or anger towards the governments and corporates who perpetuate them.

For indigenous peoples with a deep connection to and identification with the land, animals and plants, this grief is profound, and also has a practical aspect, as they see hunting lands depleted by habitat loss or climate change, water supplies diverted for "civilisation" in cities and sacred lands developed without sensitivity to their meaning and connection.

One way this grief can be harnessed is if the rage or awareness it provokes can be channelled into positive action to protect the land and reverse some of the damage already caused. It may also generate a sense of togetherness as a community, that was maybe dispersing under the pressures of modern life, but rallies to protect its surroundings.

Other people's grief

As we develop our own relationship with our own death and dying, we are likely to encounter the deaths of others along the way.

Saying the right thing

These are never easy situations, but they are all an opportunity to understand more, to explore our discomfort and to show compassion to others.

> "I just didn't know what to say to Julia! It's so awful. I mean, what can you say to someone who loses a child like that?"

> "I know, it's terrible. Poor thing. So what did you do?"

> "Well I don't think she'd seen me, so I just left the shop without speaking to her."

Sadly this experience, described here by Lucia, is a very common situation. Very obviously sad for the bereaved person who probably needs all the support and connection they can get – and sad for the friend who believes she cannot find a way to be present. These many small disconnects are often mentioned by the bereaved as a key component of their suffering.

Our human instinct is to shy away from pain. Our own of course, as well as that of others. It is an uncomfortable thing to witness. We often see that at the deathbed, expressed as an urge to sedate the dying person rather than witness their anguish. And we see it in confessions like Lucia's where she found it unbearable to confront Julia's pain and her own helplessness in alleviating it.

This behaviour is also a symptom of our urge to fix things the way we have been trained since a very early age. It can be very satisfying to be with a child who is crying or upset and to manage to soothe them and make them feel better. Our ego loves that sensation. Much less comfortable is seeing someone in deep anguish and not being able to help. It is confusing. If we can't help, says our ego, what are we doing here? What are we for? We feel inadequate. It can feel better, easier to just back away.

The truth is we often won't know if our presence is helping or not. But it might be. It might be that Julia would have had a small shred of comfort in an authentic connection with another human. An acknowledgement of her pain. One that doesn't expect anything of her but just reaches out a compassionate hand. An awareness of her suffering.

There is no magic phrase that Lucia could have come up with that would fix her friend. This is a terrible situation that will take a long time – maybe all of Julia's life – to find a way to come to terms with. So that is not a reasonable ambition for the conversation. Yet we feel that there must be something 'perfect' to say. And we are disappointed in ourselves for not finding it.

Small wonder that cliches and sentimental verses on cards are such a common resort, a substitute for the raw emotion we might feel if we went inside our hearts and connected, face to face with the other person's grief.

As anyone who has been in deep grief knows, words can seem barely relevant. Just shapes of noises. But the feeling, the energy from the other person, is very real. A few clumsy heartfelt words can bring more comfort than the automatic recital of set phrases or platitudes. Or no words at all. Just a hug, a hand on an arm, a look of compassion.

Allowing grief to run its course

As the immediate shock period passes, people who have been bereaved for more than 3 months tell me of the social pressure they feel under to be "ok" now. They feel they have overdone the expectation of sympathy, that others are no longer interested in supporting them, that they should be "getting over it".

This idea makes no sense to them if the loss is still the uppermost thing in their minds most of the time. Everyday concerns and chitchat seem staggeringly trivial. In their world, which is caving in all around them, how could they be interested in somebody's difficulty in choosing the right shade of green for a sweater? Or worrying about the bus being a bit late?

To make things more complex still, there are times when we need a rest from grief. We cannot be in that place every minute of the day. It helps if we remember that it is still ok to laugh, to enjoy a moment. Being distracted for a while does not reduce the importance of the person who has died or diminish their death. It is part of life, part of surviving loss, and part of rebuilding, reconfiguring a life without that person. It is important and healing. So sometimes a silly conversation about choosing the right shade of green sweater might be a welcome relief for the grieving person.

The truth of it is we just don't know. We don't know if reaching out a hand will invoke tenderness or irritation. We don't know what's best for the other person moment by moment. So we can start by letting go of that idea. We don't know and we cannot be expected to know.

Compassionate presence

Let's focus instead on what we *can* do. And it all comes down to compassionate presence. Holding space for the other person and whatever emotions they are feeling – tenderly, lightly, truly.

It's one thing to accept this in our minds of course, but it can be an unfamiliar process in modern life, so how do we go about it?

Like so many ways to be with others, we need first to learn how to be that with ourselves. To hold compassionate space for ourselves.

Take a deep breath and imagine a situation – maybe like Lucia's – where you have felt too uncomfortable to reach out to another person. Where you avoided them, or the subject and breathed a sigh of relief when the risk of painful conversation is over for the moment.

First consider how being in that state of awkwardness feels physically for you. Where do you feel the tension of it in your body? Does your throat tighten up? Is your jaw clenching? Your stomach cramping? How does your body react to the discomfort of the moment?

Next, listen to what the voices in your head are saying. Are they admonishing you for being a bad friend? Being too stupid to know what to say? Being a coward? A flake? An emotional cripple? Is your ego pointing out a repeating pattern?

> "This is so typical of you, you're just a fair-weather friend. You're useless at the tough stuff."

> "Tom would know what to say. What's your problem? You're just not good enough."

Or making it all about you:

> "It's not good for you to be near tragedy like this, you know you'll get upset. She'll understand why you can't be there for her. It's fine to just walk away and look after yourself. You've got enough of your own stuff to worry about."

Now press the pause button. Settle your feet onto the ground, sit up straight and take a couple of slow, deep breaths. Feel your own pain and confusion. Hold space for yourself. Accept your feelings whatever they are. Acknowledge that you are only human. As my spirit guides told me recently:

> "We LOVE it when you make mistakes!" I was shocked by their declaration. What kind of cruel mockery was this?

> "We love it because every time you make a mistake you can learn something. Grow. Evolve. Make more mistakes! Go for it!"

You might try holding that stance with yourself. Be calm in yourself, take your time before you say anything, and don't be a perfectionist. Just be there, true in your heart. Trusting that the other person will feel that and benefit from it.

Our own grief

In these situations and others, including mourning the death of someone we feel connected to, grief is a strong experience. It tests us and our inner resources. It pulls feelings out of us that we may not have acknowledged before. It can destroy all our self-control and carefully managed behaviours in one fell swoop. It may seem to have left us in peace and then come roaring back at the most unexpected and inopportune moments. It is a fierce beast.

Grief is also what shamans would call a *worthy opponent*. Meaning it is like the martial arts teacher who pushes us to our limits so that we can strengthen and improve our skills. The Moriarty to Sherlock Holmes. The Joker to Batman. Goliath to Samson. George Chuvalo to Muhammed Ali. We all have characters in our lives that offer these opportunities. They may present as enemies or rivals. They drive us nuts and leave us ragged but, in the end, we grow because of them.

So it is with grief. Nobody would wish that pain on anyone, but it does bring its gifts. Clarification, resilience, the need to develop new skills. Joan Halifax, Buddhist nun and pioneer of palliative care and accompanying people during death put it like this:

> *"Grief can seem like an unbearable experience. But for those of us who have entered the broken world of loss and sorrow, we realize that in the fractured landscape of grief we can find the pieces of our life that we ourselves have forgotten... grief and sorrow may teach us gratitude for what we have been given, even the gift of suffering"*
> Joan Halifax, Upaya Zen (Halifax)

Grief as a Force for Change

In 1993, Doreen Lawrence (Wikipedia, n.d.) and her husband Neville lost their teenage son when he was murdered in a racist attack in London, England. That was already a tragedy, but the Lawrences felt – and it has subsequently been acknowledged – that the case was handled in an unbalanced way, under-investigating the six white men who killed Stephen. This landmark tragedy is still referred to in the efforts to rid the London police service (Metropolitan Police) of racist individuals and biases.

Losing a son is enough to generate a terrible sense of loss. This is further compounded when there is violence involved and then a lack of justice. Doreen Lawrence, now a Baroness and named by the BBC radio program Woman's Hour as Britain's Most Influential Woman in 2014, could have collapsed under that grief, but instead she founded the Stephen Lawrence Charitable Trust and has been a tireless anti-racism campaigner and spokesperson since then.

What I do not want to say here though, is that there is a correct way to grieve. Or that it is in any way an easy process. Maybe the most important message about grief is allowing. Allowing the grieving person – including ourselves if it is us - to process in their own way. The more accepting we are as a society, that grief is a natural and necessary part of accepting change, the more people will feel able to express their grief in healthy ways rather than bottle it up or redirect it into rage or longer lasting mental or physical health issues.

We all grieve differently to each other. We even grieve differently to ourselves from one day to the next. Someone experiencing grief may find themselves laughing hysterically, working like a maniac, collapsed sobbing on the bathroom floor, eating chocolate all day or shutting themselves away from a world "which doesn't understand". All in the space of a few days. When grief is filling our hearts and minds, it can seem unimaginable that the rest of the world is fussing about which kind of latte to have or who won last night's football match. Our whole being is so flooded with grief that many things seem irrelevant.

The allowing can be all round. Allowing people with different cultural traditions to do things their way. Allowing people to deviate from their cultural traditions. Allowing ourselves to be rubbish at things we normally do well. Allowing the grieving person time. Allowing them to be alright one day and not the next. Allowing them to take as long as they need.

And, when you are the grieving person, maybe you can find it in your heart to allow the rest of us to get it wrong. To not understand, to fail to make you feel better, to say the wrong thing - that acceptance also helps all of us learn and grow.

Helping someone who is grieving

What not to do

As we already considered, a common experience of bereaved people is their friends avoiding them. And the usual explanation those friends give, is not knowing what to say.

This is a terrible blight on our society, that we think there are the perfect words for every occasion. Of course there are the formulaic options:

"I'm so sorry for your loss."

"I heard about your father".

They can feel genuine or trite. It's all in the delivery.

Part of the problem is that we feel there might be some words that will help ease their pain. It's like a test. If we come up with the magic password, then everything will be alright. So start by letting go of that idea. Nothing you say is going to make everything alright. They are in their grieving process, and it hurts. If it is early in the process they may also be in shock, be overwhelmed, be emotionally paralysed or unable to give voice to their feelings. If the death was some time ago, they may feel they are no longer *allowed* to talk about it, that they are supposed to have "got over it" by now and be "Moving on!".

But there are no timetables on grief. One person might lose themselves in getting on with things, preferring to meter out their grief in small doses, while another might throw themselves headlong into their feelings and responses, no matter the social niceties.

One of the earliest funerals I remember attending, when I was about 12, was for a young man whose new wife had died of a brain tumour. He was a big, burly fellow but he couldn't even stand at the funeral. His friends had to help him down the aisle in the church. He sobbed and wailed all the way through. This was England in the 1970s where emotions were rarely expressed and never in front of a church full of friends, family and strangers. The rest of the people there were either shocked or moved, depending on their point of view. I was astonished. I'd never seen an adult cry, I don't think I even realised men were "allowed" to cry, and certainly not in such a wholehearted way. It was deeply affecting and still moves me to tears when I remember it all these years later.

What might help

So what can we do? Well for one thing, we can find it in ourselves to approach those who are mourning. You don't even have to say anything. A hand on an arm, a hug, a cup of tea. All sorts of things can help a little without needing magic words. The worst is to do nothing. To abandon them when they may already feel abandoned by the person who has died.

A good start can be to simply acknowledge their loss. It is the biggest thing on their mind, and it may help them to hear that you are aware of that. It can be more helpful to accept the unique nature of their grief, than to say you know how they are feeling or start talking about your own bereavements.

> "I can't imagine what you are going through."

Often, I see people earnestly offering to help – anything, just ask. The offer is sincere and heartfelt. But often a bereaved person is in no fit state to manage such open-ended offers. It just swirls into the overwhelm and disappears without trace. Unless, maybe, you know them well enough to be more targeted and practical about your offer.

> "Would it help if I popped round later to take the dog for a walk?"

> "I know Freda did all the driving; I'm going to the supermarket, so I'll pick you up some stuff ok?"

> "I've got a printer; do you need a hand with things for the funeral?"

Compassionate presence is, as ever, one of the best tools you have at your disposal. People will often feel exhausted and overwhelmed by grief so be gentle with your offers of company.

> "I'll sit with you for a bit, we don't need to talk"

Another common experience can be that nobody wants to mention the person who has died. Not realising that the bereaved person may want to talk of little else. Sharing stories of the person who has passed on is common at wakes after a funeral – often the more outrageous stories coming out as the drinking progresses if it's that sort of event.

Storytelling to grieve

The Shona people, who live in Zimbabwe and parts of Mozambique, have a beautiful tradition of storytelling about the person who has died. They come together as a community and share stories that highlight different aspects of the person. The man we knew as our father may have characteristics we never appreciated, that have been seen by his partner or best friends. Together these different perspectives are considered and incorporated, until in the end, the community has a clear idea of the person. It might be refreshingly honest, and it is a shared view, reached by consensus. Since honouring the ancestors is very important, as it is in most indigenous communities, it matters what this new ancestor is to be known for. They might call on legendary warriors in one moment or those known for their deep wisdom or kindness or creativity in another. This way the community has a kind of catalogue of ancestors and their special attributes, as well as having had a chance to share all their favourite stories at this special time.

A Western version of this might be to go through all the old photos you have of someone's life to make a reel for the funeral or an album to share with friends. There could be video clips too and maybe certificates or newspaper clippings. Rather than including everything you find, you might discuss with those involved what they think are the most important characteristics of the person and focus on things which illustrate those.

Regret

Allow space for regret in grief. There can be regret for harsh words shared – especially if that was the last interaction with the person who has died. Words never spoken which could have been so precious. Regret for missed opportunities, the failure to visit as often as possible, even what George Orwell would term "thought crimes" – those moments when our own human frailty has us thinking unkind, spiteful or hateful things about someone who has now gone.

In our Sacred Death course, we write letters to those people who have died and with whom we feel we could have said or done things better. The unsaid words, the words we wish we hadn't said, the things we did and didn't do. Writing all this in a letter to the person who has died – however long ago – can be a way to release some of this regret, acknowledging what we already know, that what's done is done, and allowing everybody to move on. As I have experienced in some of the shamanic sessions I have carried out for people, these regrets act as chains for the dead as well as for the living. See if you can find a way to let those regrets go and let's all enjoy a more expansive sense of freedom.

Models of Grief

"Be full of sorrow, that you may become hill of joy; weep, that you may break into laughter."

"What hurts you, blesses you. Darkness is your candle." Rumi, mystic poet

While acknowledging that every loss is different, and each person's reaction to it will have its own nuance, it can sometimes help those in grief to understand some of the theories or models of grief that have been researched and studied by others. We will look at three of these here. If this is an area that interests you there is a lot more material available, including some great content on the Good Grief YouTube channel.

5 stages of grief (Kübler-Ross model)

Many of us will have heard of the classic 5 stages of grief first outlined by hospice pioneer Elisabeth Kübler-Ross in her landmark book On Death and Dying (Ross, 1969). It is important to note that this is not a prescriptive list. There is no set time a person might spend on each stage, and they may not follow this order at all. They may also lurch back and forth between stages. However it can help those in the grief process – or someone supporting a person who is – to at least be aware of the stages.

Denial and Isolation

Many will start here. Especially if the death is sudden or unexpected. Even people I have worked with who have spent a year tending to their dying parent can experience this kind of disbelief when they die. Our brains struggle to make sense of this total absence of the other person. Floundering and overwhelmed, it may feel essential to avoid contact with anyone else – worrying that other people they might not understand, or they might try to fix things.

Someone else might throw themselves into the practical arrangements as a way of avoiding the reality of their pain. "Being brave" and focusing on funerals, sharing the news, consoling others can feel noble and courageous, allowing us to postpone the beginning of our own grief journey.

There can be lingering versions of this for many years when the bereaved struggle to clear out possessions, or leave their child's bedroom, exactly as it was. Some part of them still struggles to accept the truth.

Anger

A common reaction, especially to the death of a spouse or close family member is anger. This could be directed at the person who has died:

>   *How could you leave me like this?*

>   *How could you have been so stupid?*

>   *Why didn't you see the car coming?*

Or at the disease they died from or the doctors who have apparently failed to save them. It can also be directed inwards if there is guilt around the death or the state of the relationship with the person who has died. The fire of anger may burn through us, helping us adjust and let go of those beliefs and ideas that no longer serve us.

Bargaining

In some ways bargaining seems like an inappropriate reaction. Unless the grief is pre-emptive (the kind of grief that is felt prior to the person dying, when death is known to be a likely outcome in the short term), and it may feel essential to spend all the family's life savings on a possible cure.

Please God, save them. I'll do whatever you want.

Bargaining can also be a stage of grief after someone's death. Maybe praying constantly or developing new habits to assuage guilt.

Depression

A profound sense of sadness, leaving someone feeling hopeless and unable to participate in everyday life, is normal for a while. There's no getting away from the pain of grief. But sometimes the bereaved can get stuck here and need professional support to emerge and start to rebuild a new version of their life.

Acceptance

This is a goal, but it may not be available to everybody. Or may take a long time to achieve. It is not to be confused with getting over the death. The loss of someone is a lifelong experience which won't go away with time. What can happen though is that enough other life experiences cushion the loss, making it easier to live with.

Sixth stage of grief

Some grief experts also talk about a sixth stage, that of "finding meaning". Someone who can accomplish this has been able to see the lessons they have learned from the other person, from their interactions with them, maybe also from their death. It is not obvious to all how finding positive benefits from such a difficult event would even be possible, and as such, is not as universally accepted as the first 5 stages.

The Fried Egg model

Another way of considering this is the so-called Fried Egg model of grief developed by New Zealand based Grief Counsellor Lois Tonkin (Tonkin, 1996)

Tonkin considers that rather than our grief diminishing, our life grows around it – her approach is described as Growing around Grief in the article she wrote where she first suggested this idea.

She was inspired by a client who talked about how at first, the death of her child filled her entire sense of being. And that she had expected that gradually, given enough time, this grief would diminish. Her actual experience was more that the grief stayed the same, while a buffer zone gradually grew around it – much like when we first put an egg in a frying pan, and all we can see is the yolk (the grief) but then gradually the white appears around it.

The four tasks of grief

Psychologist William Worden feels that these models might be too passive and that in fact the grieving person has work to do, rather than just waiting for stages to pass. In his book Grief Counseling and Grief Therapy (Worden, 2018), he talks about the four tasks of grief:

1. **Accept the reality of the loss**
    Some denial is usual at first. I heard only today, of a small child killed in an accident a few weeks ago. Her parents

didn't attend the cremation. Denial provides a buffer, some space to adjust to the shock. The healing process can start when the person has stepped out of denial. It might be a good reason to delay the cremation or funeral if it is in a country or culture where that is an acceptable option.

2. **Experience the pain of grief**
"Big boys don't cry"
"Chin up"
"Time to pull yourself together"
Our Western society has not given us good tools for feeling, expressing or releasing emotion. But we know better now, and those feelings – however painful – will exist whether we allow them to or not. The only difference is if we feel them, we can work with them and through them. The alternative is to stuff them down inside our bodies where they will cause us further harm.

3. **Adjust to an environment with the deceased missing**
Lots of things are different after the loss of a loved one. Many people tell me it takes them years to stop thinking "Oh I must tell…. about that, they'd laugh their head off" or "That's a perfect sweater for him, I must buy it". Practical adjustments, strategic adjustments maybe, like moving home, social adjustments (do keep inviting your bereaved friends, even if they keep saying no. They may be terrified to go to a social event alone after decades of having a partner but don't give up on them) or the heartache of cooking for one or sleeping alone. The adjustments are numerous and will sometimes feel too much to bear. Finding new ways to be in the world is part of the work.

4. **Find an Enduring Connection with the Deceased While Embarking on a New Life**
Between the unhealthy choices of obsession with the departed person or acting like they never existed, lies this

world of shaping a new form of connection with them. A way to be able to move on to the next part of one's life, bringing all that was learnt and shared with the person who has died. It might involve creating a memory book about them for instance, or sharing stories the way the Shona people do to identify the core characteristics of the person who has died. And it includes creating your new life.

Complex Grief

It is totally natural and necessary to grieve our losses. We must come to terms with a change in the way our world is organised. The most difficult part of this process is usually in the first 3-6 months after the death, though as I have said, each of us is different and there's no right or wrong way forward.

In some cases though, someone might get into a state known as complex grief, where they are not showing signs of coming to terms with the death or rebuilding their life without the person who has died. That may be enough to destroy their own will to live.

I visited a river in Northern Uganda where we saw the local species of eagle who nested high in the clifftops around the river. The guide explained that they mated for life, and that when one or other of the pair died, the surviving one would hurl itself from the top of the cliff, plummeting to its death on the rocks below. It seemed they were not prepared to continue without each other, and this happens sometimes with couples.

One man I knew spent several years as sole carer for his wife when she developed Multiple Sclerosis. He adapted their house for her wheelchair and, thanks to his nursing training, was able to take care of most of her needs at home. When she died there in her 50s, we thought he would at last have some respite from this physically and emotionally strenuous responsibility. But he never recovered from her death and died himself within a year.

A Danish study (Alexandros Katsiferis, 2023) looked at just under one million citizens aged 65 and over who lost their spouse. Interestingly, the younger they were at the time of widowhood, the stronger the impact on life expectancy. Gender also played a role with men 70% more likely to die in the first year of widowhood than other men their age.

Complex grief is more likely to occur if the death is sudden or involves violence (eg suicide or murder). It is also more likely if the death is a child of the person grieving or a long-term partner or if the person grieving has complicating pre-existent mental health issues.

Of course grief is always hard. But complex grief can have a long-term impact on someone's quality of life for an extended period. They may have difficulty accepting the death, climbing out of depression or rebuilding a new life for themselves. In this case of persistent and intense grief, professional help from a specialised therapist of grief counsellor is recommended.

It may also help to join a specialist support group. A friend of mine found great solace from the group that he joined for partners of suicides. He felt able to express some of his own guilt and shame that he had held inside since his wife's death, feeling like those in his normal community were probably already blaming him or holding him accountable for not managing to stop her. He had no prior experience of this kind of tragedy and no idea how to process his complicated and contradictory feelings.

Misunderstood grief

An under-recognised aspect of grief is any situation when the bereaved person is not expected to be very upset. They may then be denied the opportunity to express their grief or receive support from those around them.

Lovers

This situation can arise for example in the case of a secret love affair.

I know of one woman whose secret lover of 32 years died unexpectedly of a heart attack. She didn't even know when it happened – since she was a secret then of course nobody would think to tell her. All she knew was that he suddenly stopped answering her messages. Even if she had known, it would have been difficult for his family if she had gone to the funeral.

In fact the funeral had already happened when she found out a few weeks later, via mutual contacts. She had already gone through the heartbreak of suddenly losing contact after all that time, wondering and then starting to come to terms with the end of the relationship, only to discover the truth and experience the grief of losing him without the possibility of taking some comfort from the customary procedures of death.

It can help in that situation to arrange your own funeral. You don't need a body for it, and you don't need to follow any of the usual norms. She could create a meaningful ceremony that would be very personal to her and her lover.

Difficult and former partners

When I discovered that my first husband, long since divorced, had died, I was completely thrown. At one level I had chosen to end the marriage and hadn't seen or heard from him for nearly 30 years. On the other he had been part of my life, my journey and the news that he had died, and I hadn't even known, felt like a blow.

I felt the need to carry out my own farewell ceremony for him, particularly as I had no idea of the nature of his premature death. I wanted to make sure he was alright and had passed on. During the ceremony it came up that we did have some unfinished business. He wanted my forgiveness for his violent response to the end of our marriage, and I wanted his for the pain I had caused him. We made our peace and his spirit moved on.

I remember as a child being surprised when a woman I knew, who had always had a bitter and difficult relationship with her husband, was very upset by his death. It made no sense to me at the time. Isn't she better off without him? I thought. Yet these people are still part of the framework of our lives and living without them is an adjustment – even if their death is in many ways either a relief or of no practical impact.

Death of a Pet

Those who have not been pet owners can find it hard to relate to the depth of grief that someone can feel when they lose their faithful friend. Many people form very close bonds with their pets and can be devastated by their loss. They may see the pet as their best friend, their confidant, maybe even their life partner.

Others who have not experienced this bond, can take what feels like a harsh view - as though the beloved cat or dog was only a commodity.

"Are you going to get another one?"

If you or someone you know has suffered the loss of their faithful companion, it is an important time to show compassion. For yourself if you are the one who is grieving – just like the loss of a human, you may want to create a memorial, reminisce about your pet, or create a memento, for example from their ashes, if that brings you comfort.

If it is someone you know who has suffered this loss, then hold space in your heart for their grief – even if it makes no sense to you. Just as we can never understand the full depth of a relationship between two humans, we may never fully know the role the animal played in that person's life. So be generous with your compassion, acknowledge their feelings and allow them safe space to feel them.

A more positive aspect to this kind of loss though can be that for other people, talking about the death of a pet is more manageable territory than human loss. A friend shared that he had a lot more conversations with friends who asked about the death of his dog than about the death of his father. It may be because this is seen as more straightforward kind of grief – one where the animal is much loved and was always likely to die before its owner without the possible emotional complexities of a parent-child or other human-human relationship.

Celebrities

Celebrity deaths are another example of grief that might not be expected or well thought of by those around the grieving person. The collective grief after the death of the 36-year-old Princess Diana was a shock to many. So much for the British tradition of a stiff upper lip. It is estimated that one million bouquets of flowers were left outside her home in Kensington Palace, and three million gathered in the streets on the day of her funeral. Estimates are that a further 2.5 billion people worldwide watched it on TV. This attractive young mother had captivated many people, and the nature of her death added to the sense of drama. In the weeks and months after the funeral, suicide rates among those most identified with her (women of a similar age) went up by 45%.

Much has been written about what some journalists and commentators described as "mass hysteria" following her death. She was hugely popular and many sympathised with her story. One theory is that for many she represented a more modern version of the British Royal Family. A more compassionate, expressive and relatable version. So the grief was not only for the woman Diana, but also for all the hope of change that she represented, which felt dashed by her death.

We have had a small glimpse of the vast landscape of grief and grieving. On reflection, my key message to you here is that we can't dodge grief or skip over it, it's tough and as a society, the better able we become to feel our way through and stand in compassionate presence with each other through the storm, the better off we will all be. No formula, no rules, no judgement.

Section 7: Planning your perfect death

Overview

This can be a confusing area which few people have the urge to deal with – and then may be put off by complexities. Yet over and over I see difficult situations that could have been made easier for the dying person and those around them if End-of-Life Planning had been addressed. I urge you to keep reading and then, even better, to put your plan in place, whatever your age and state of health.

End-of-Life Planning is an important topic that is very often neglected. For instance, only about a third of US or European citizens living in care homes or the equivalent have completed an Advance Directive stating their preferences around death and dying. Of the overall population the completion rate is likely to be significantly lower.

The UK End-of-Life Doula Association, with whom I trained and have my professional membership, talk about a Planning Umbrella which can make it easier to understand.

This Planning Umbrella for End-of-Life includes four elements:

1. **What I want during dying process**: my wishes and preferences
2. **What I don't want during dying process:** my view on interventions such as resuscitation or life support
3. **My Spokesperson?** my nominated spokesperson who would speak for me if I were no longer able.

4. **My After death wishes**: How I would like my body cared for? Funeral Arrangements, Will, digital will, organ / tissue / whole body donation

However, it is important that you find out about End-of-Life Plan options in your own country, or the country in which you currently are living. The rules can vary a lot from one jurisdiction to the other, even from state to state in Australia or the USA.

Whatever the legal situation though, I urge you to start by thinking through what you really want, in an ideal world, accepting that it might turn out quite differently.

Until you have an idea about this, and then share it with those who need to know, any other details are less important. If at the very least you have a statement stating your position and in which situations you do not consider life prolonging measures to be in your best interests, then at least those close to you, and any medics taking decisions on your behalf, will have something to go on rather than just guessing and following standard protocol.

You don't need to wait until you have all the answers. Just make a start. It can get more complete over time and there may be things you want to change later, for example, to align your life stage or treatment options. All of that is possible, we just need to make a start.

End-of-Life Planning

Note that because the terminology is different in different countries, and may have varying legal standing in different jurisdictions, I am going to use the phrase "End-of-Life Plan" as a generic term meaning some form of document that you have created to share your wishes with others.

What is an End-of-Life Plan about?

An End-of-Life Plan, sometimes called an Advance Directive or Living Will, is, simply put, how you would like your End-of-Life care to look. It will include big decisions like Do Not Resuscitate (DNR) or DNACPR (Do /not administer CPR) and can also cover as much information as you like around comfort, treatment preferences and personal care - from how you like your tea to who you want to be present at the end.

There are lots of reasons why this End-of-Life Plan doesn't get done. Most of us assume (and often hope) our death is a good way off, so it isn't high on our list of priorities. Though of course none of us know when the unexpected will strike, and if we were suddenly to – for example – have an accident or illness that left us unable to communicate, then it would be better for everyone, including ourselves, to understand our wishes and have a clear communication of them.

Sometimes avoidance is superstitious. The sense that planning one's own death will somehow hasten it. Of course we don't think that rationally, but there is a fear and tendency to avoid the subject. There can also be fear of creating something set in stone.

> "What if I change my mind?"

It's important to know that these documents can be amended or added to throughout our life. Every day if you like. We are not making a permanent commitment to one thing. Many of us feel differently about quality-of-life issues for example, as life progresses. What may seem unbearable to a healthy, fit 25-year-old may turn out to be tolerable as our capacities gradually decline towards the end of our life.

A friend of mine who works with head trauma shared with me that one of the biggest factors in how well patients recover is whether or not they accept their injury and the subsequent impact on their physical and mental capacities. Until they have done that, they can't begin to work with what capacities they now have and improve the situation as much as they can.

Keeping your End-of-Life Plan up to date

It's important to be aware that your End-of-Life Plan is always your current best idea of what you will want. It is your document about your End-of-Life and under your capacity to change, provided you are still able to do so. Of course there are some checks and balances in the system to avoid manipulation of the dying.

In fact it makes absolute sense to review it from time to time as you proceed through your life. Maybe you wrote it when you were single and childless but now you have a partner and children, things could feel different. Maybe you have shifted your views about hospital medicine during the last few years and would like to update some of your wishes. Or advances in medicine or symptom management change the balance and would lead you to a different choice now.

We all evolve and change in the course of our lives and while this shouldn't become a source of constant worry and administrative effort, it is worth checking in with yourself say once a decade, or after a significant change in circumstances, to see if anything needs an update.

The legal process and status of End-of-Life Plans varies by country, and over time, so I highly recommend you check how they work where you live. Even if they have no legal standing however, they can be valuable input to those responsible for your care.

Start with what you want

A good way to make the task feel more manageable is to start not with official paperwork, but with thinking about what YOU want. What matters to you.

Here are some of the questions you could consider when deciding what feels right for your End-of-Life Plan. Bear in mind that this plan is your ideal scenario. As anybody who has made a Birth Plan knows, we must be ready for anything and open to the fact that things may not turn out as we expected.

Nonetheless, it is still valuable to accept the uncertainties and still think things through and define your preferences. If you believe in the Law of Attraction, then designing your perfect death could make it more likely to turn out that way.

Many of us have the habit of pushing aside our own needs in the interests of "being nice", "being good" or avoiding conflict.

One of my own cases of this, before I did my End-of-Life Doula training, was when I missed a flight to the UK because I popped into the airport clinic to check out some heart arrhythmia and ended up being wheeled out on a stretcher, with a drip, into a waiting ambulance. I was conscious and not in pain, so kept apologising to the people who had to get out of the way. Once in the ambulance the paramedics declared me the most cheerful person they had ever taken to hospital.

Of course some of that was my own coping mechanism. I certainly did not want to die alone in the middle of the night thousands of miles from home, which at the time felt like a very real possibility. I was shocked by the fact that the first my kids would hear about it when they woke up the next day was that it was all over. So I plastered a lot of good cheer and jolliness over the top of my concerns. And completely disregarded my own needs.

I hope that I've learnt my lesson now and am more alert to the option of asserting my own preferences – in life as well as in death.

Writing something in your End-of-Life Plan doesn't guarantee things will work out that way… but it's more likely than if nobody even knows what you want.

Writing your End-of-Life Plan

As one self-development organisation I have worked with would say:

> "Ask for exactly what you want and then be prepared to negotiate."

So here are some suggestions of things you might want to think about defining.

Overall position

It can be useful to begin by defining your own personal idea of the dying process. How you feel about it. Here are a few extracts that might get you started:

> "Having a conscious death is very important to me. I would like to be as present as possible and have the time and space to create a sacred moment that fills me with peace."

> "I want my dying to be like my living – full of life and colour. Let's get as many visitors there as possible, make the most of our time together, share memories and express our feelings."

> "I have a very difficult relationship with my family. I really don't want them around at the end of my life bringing all their drama into the situation. I'd just like to be with my guru, my two closest friends and my own thoughts."

With that in mind, let's look in more detail at what we might include in our own End-of-Life Plan

Details

Location

Where would you choose to end your life? Some people feel reassured by hospitals and knowing they have access to the best medical care. Others may prefer the homeliness of being in their own bed with their family on hand. Hospice deaths have become more common in many countries for those dying of longer-term diseases. Think about what really matters for you. Do you prefer the more personal experience of not being surrounded by the busyness of a hospital or would you find being with your family too intensely personal?

Some people have a very clear idea that they want to go home to their origins, or to a favourite location away from everyone. And why not? This is their death, and they have every right to decide where it should take place.

I was surprised when I was making my first birth plan how important it felt to me to be able to get straight into my own bed with my new-born baby. To listen to my own music and sit on my own toilet. It had to be a home birth for me. This is not everybody's choice and the important thing here is to tune into what we really want. There is no right and wrong way to die. We all have different priorities.

People

Maybe this is obvious to you, and you'd want just your partner, or all your close family and friends around you at the end of your life. Others might choose a more reflective end with time and space to contemplate or to rest. Again try to focus on what is right for you, especially if you have a history of being a people pleaser. Maybe this is the one time in your life when it's going to be all about you and what will give you the best chance of a comfortable and peaceful death.

And there are others to think about. Do you want any religious practitioners or healers around? Your accountant? Your therapist? Your dog? Would you love to have your grandchildren chattering in the corner or do you think the deathbed is no place for children?

Maybe there are particular friends in your life who you know would be perfect company in this moment. So many of us feel we cannot ask for things for ourselves, but maybe this is the one time you can. Maybe that friend would be honoured to know that you wanted them near at such an important time.

Environment

Have a think too about the room and any information you could share with whoever will be there so they can make you as comfortable as possible. I'm a fresh air fiend so it would be important for me to have an open window, or even to be outside if the weather permitted. The hospice I volunteered in during my training had some rooms with balconies and terraces that patients' beds could be wheeled out onto on fine days. They could hear the birdsong, smell the flowers, enjoy the sky.

I don't like muggy heat, but I also hate a cold draught. Pernickety, eh? But surely this is the one time in your life you can have everything the way you want it.

Ever since someone gave me a silk pillowcase a few years ago I have loved them and would hope to feel that next to my face. I have strong views on colours so would want to be surrounded by supportive colours - of course that would be taken care of in my own home, but even in hospital it should be possible to bring in a blanket or scarf that will make you feel better.

Clutter can make me feel agitated so I'd like things to be kept tidy around me – but also to have easy access to anything I might want quickly, like a glass of water or my phone.

What about you? If you imagine your perfect deathbed scene, how is the room? Pot plants? Fresh flowers? Muslin curtains blowing in the breeze or snug and centrally heated? Do you like natural light or a low-level lamp?

Maybe if you are bed-bound you'd like photographs of friends, family, your life, stuck to the ceiling above your bed to give you a feast of happy memories to survey.

Entertainment

Are you one of those people who puts the TV or radio on as soon as you get home? Maybe even if you're not actively watching or listening you like the chatter, the sense of not being alone.

Or you could be the kind of person who loves silence, space to think, peace and quiet.

Personally I like to listen to audio books – even though I don't enjoy someone reading a book out loud to me. Other people I have worked with to create their End-of-Life Plan are the opposite.

It might be worth creating a list of your preferences. TED talks or comedy? Classical music or prog rock? Spiritual readings or soap operas? You can always change your mind of course, as with everything else, but you may as well have a starting point. Maybe create a playlist, stock up on audio books or subscribe to podcasts.

Food and Drink

It may well be that you are not at all interested in eating towards the end of your life. But in the last months before that stage you may still have some appetite – why not enjoy eating and drinking your favourite things?

You may have food preferences such as vegan, gluten free, a love of spicy food, a strong urge for pudding after every meal - that carers might not be aware of, but which could make a big difference to your physical comfort and your appetite.

Think about the kind of foods you crave when you are under the weather. Hearty soups? Comfort foods full of warmth? Chocolate and sweet things? A cup of your favourite brand of coffee made with oat milk and brown sugar?

Go for it, specify everything you'd love. Maybe you will get it and maybe not. When I was in hospital visiting a friend's father, who was rapidly losing weight in the last three months of his life, and ordering food for him because he was asleep or not interested, I wished I had known more about what he would be likely to feel like eating.

I had information from the medical staff about choosing soft foods, but I hadn't known him long enough to know what his favourite dishes were. It would have been helpful to consult a document with that kind of information. Likewise if I had known enough to put something on the headphones that he would enjoy listening to, or what magazines he might like, I would have felt I could have been more helpful to him.

Spokesperson

You may feel that others know you well enough to speak for you. This can be the case, but it is worth considering that they are likely to be distressed and under a lot of pressure. Nobody wants to be the one to say no, so it can be a kindness to be clear.

Officially nominating your spokesperson is more likely to be respected or recognised in some countries than others but it is still a useful step. Depending on where you live, your chosen person may not have the right to say no to interventions, if for example they are your long-term partner, but you are not legally married. Or your dying friend may come from a different culture where their parents have very different views to the ones you know your friend now holds. Who gets the final say? Do you want that scope for uncertainty, fear, guilt or resentment during your dying process? Probably not. So worth having a spokesperson.

Medical Procedures

An important aspect of your death plan is medical interventions. What are you happy having and what would you resist, when you are in a life-threatening situation or unable to make your wishes known - for example, because you are unconscious or cannot speak or in another country and don't have the language?

Section 7: Planning your perfect death…Writing your End-of-Life Plan

We all have different levels of pain tolerance and differing ideas about what interventions we are comfortable with.

I had never known I had an issue with blood transfusions until my midwife asked me if I wanted to have one after haemorrhaging a considerable amount of blood during the birth of my second child. It was only when faced with the idea of somebody else's blood in my body that I realised I'd rather not. Luckily in this situation I had the option of rehydrating and two weeks of bed rest. I'm not saying I would refuse a blood transfusion if it would save my life, I'm just sharing that these decisions are not always clear cut.

As much as possible, try to imagine yourself into situations so you can see what you *feel* as well as what you think.

Some are easier to specify. For instance if you are on life support, at what point would you choose for your family to turn off the machines? Immediately? Never? If there was no sign of brain activity? If your priest / healer / twin brother said so? You won't be able to prescribe your wishes for every possible scenario in your plan, but the more you can say, the more information your next of kin will have on which to base their decisions, if you cannot make them for yourself.

You should also say at what point you wouldn't want any further life-saving interventions. This covers resuscitation (DNR, do not resuscitate) but you may want to include other procedures that would save your life. You may only want them if your quality of life afterwards is likely to meet certain criteria eg able to feed myself, able to recognise friends and family, able to communicate love to my children.

Bear in mind that our views on some of these things will change during our lifetime and what may seem unbearable to a healthy 35-year-old can be tolerable to someone who has experienced gradual loss of mobility or independence. This is your plan, and you can amend it whenever you want.

When considering what interventions you would choose or not choose, bear in mind this data – the result of asking doctors (who have seen more of these treatments be applied to patients) what they would choose for themselves:

- CPR (Cardiopulmonary resuscitation): 90% No
- Dialysis: 87% No
- Ventilation: 87% No
- Surgery 80% No
- Feeding Tube: 77% No
- IV Hydration: 58% No
- Pain Control: 82% Yes

In summary, pain relief is the only clear yes for Johns Hopkins educated doctors. (Radiolab.org, 2013)

It is impossible to draw up a document that covers every possible eventuality but try to at least create an overview statement that makes your general position clear.

Sample Quality of Life statement

Here is an example of such a statement, sharing your view of what "quality of life" means to you and therefore under what conditions you would not want your life to be prolonged by eg CPR, ventilator machine, feeding tube, life support.

What quality of life and/or meaningful recovery means to me

I don't want to have my life prolonged/sustained if I am no longer able to enjoy what is important to me. These are some of the aspects of life that I consider to be important and would want to be able to continue if my life was prolonged:

- To connect with others, to feel love and joy from the people I love and who love me and for them to feel they can still receive love from me.
- To be able to communicate with these people – including sometimes asking them to leave me on my own for a while.
- I want to be able to choose my food and drink – and when I have them, not to be artificially fed.
- I want to be capable of choosing how I spend my time. What I read or listen to or watch. What clothes I wear. How I do my hair.

I would *not* want my life prolonged or sustained if at least one of the following were true:

- I am unable to recognise the people I love.
- I cannot communicate with them by voice, computer, or sign language.
- I am in deep and enduring pain that cannot be treated.
- I would have to live in a care or nursing home in a condition that does not allow me to do the things described above.

Spiritual beliefs

This is a very personal area that those caring for you may not be aware of. It can also be quite finely nuanced. I was delighted to be able to tell one client living in a new country that I had tracked down an English-speaking Catholic church for her after she had told me how much comfort she got from visiting church daily where she lived before.

But it was the simple beauty of the churches in that country that had appealed to her with their cool shadows and whitewashed walls. She had no interest in going to a more ornate church. After further discussion we were able to establish that she would prefer a small altar in the room she was confined to. A side table, a white cloth, and a simple collection of a statue of Mary and some flowers, to put her in mind of those comforting visits.

In the past, many people would be dying in a community of the same religious beliefs as them, but in the multicultural transient world in which we now live, this is unlikely. So if you can, be clear about what you would like, even if it is not aligned to the religion or culture you were raised with. Let your carers know if there were holy images you would like to be able to see, or music or teachings you would like to listen to. Maybe a priest or representative of the religion to visit you.

Legal Matters

There are a few aspects to this that you may want to consider.

Will

Writing your will is an obvious first step. If your plan is simple, and in line with the defaults in your country, then if there is no will (referred to as dying intestate) than the defaults will apply.

But maybe that isn't what you want. For example you may have changed your marital status. This impacted a friend of mine whose ex-husband died prematurely in his 40s without a will, so all his money went to his new wife, leaving my friend without child support for herself and their three school age children that she was raising. This put her in a very difficult position that that the new wife was not prepared to help with. He loved his children and probably would not have wanted this to be the case but considered himself too young to need a will.

Also if you have any specific intentions such as leaving a bequest to your favourite charity, then you want to make sure they will take place.

Making a will needn't be complicated or expensive. It's nowhere near as difficult as those avoiding it might think. Joincake.com is a fabulous website that will guide you through a lot of your End-of-Life preparations and websites like bequeathed.org will even prepare your will for free.

Funeral arrangements

- What would you like to happen to your physical body when you leave it – to be an organ donor? Embalmed or not? Open or closed coffin?
- Do you have funeral preferences? Burial or cremation? Traditional or green? Coffin or calico wrap? What to do with your ashes? Music? Readings? Location? Celebrant? Style of service?
- Do you have a Legacy you wish to share? Maybe donations you want to make to a charity or cause you support? Last messages or advice for friends and family?
- How would you like to be remembered? Memorial – would you like a headstone? Style? A tree? A plaque?

- How would you like to be remembered on the anniversaries of your death?
- What about your digital assets? You can memorialise eg your Facebook account, so that the record of your life stays intact, and people can leave messages for you. digitallegacyassociation.org supports you to create a digital will for these assets and any others like crypto currency or NFTs

LPOAs

All this information can be referred to in any Lasting Powers of Attorney (LPOA) you set up. Choose carefully who you think is best fitted to the role. In the UK you have one LPOA for financial issues and one for health and well-being. They can be different people, or they can be several people. If you put your two children, are they likely to be able to come to an agreement? Or is one better at finances and one more aligned to your views on medical procedures?

Living Funeral

A few years ago I had never heard this term. Though it did cross my mind at funerals that it was a shame the person couldn't be sitting at the front enjoying all these wonderful things being said about them.

Some people would feel that the recently departed friend or relative might be doing just that, in spirit at least, but even then, it wouldn't be easy for them to respond to the words being shared or to acknowledge the beautiful emotions on display.

A Living Funeral can be a lovely way to do this and allow the person who is about to die to have full awareness of just how loved and appreciated they are – while they are still able to acknowledge and enjoy it. Maybe they too have sentiments they wish to share, advice to give, or apologies to offer.

As well as being a celebration of the person's life, this approach also gives them the opportunity to design the service that they want, rather than hoping for the best or directing others to do so when they die. On the other hand, it might be friends and family who decide to arrange the Living Funeral or Celebration of Life as a surprise gift for the person in question.

An additional benefit can be support for the closest family and friends as they manage their pre-emptive grief. When the end is approaching, and does come, the experience of the Living Funeral can generate a stronger network of people to be with them when death occurs.

Recommendation

I recommend to every single person who might die one day, in other words all of us, to create an End-of-Life Plan containing the information as described above. And anything else you want to include. You don't need to wait until death is just around the corner. In fact, it is usually better not to. Write it from the more objective stance of someone who assumes they still have a long time to go. If you can't face doing all of it, do some of it.

Make sure it is signed and dated and witnessed so that if for instance your parents / children / medical team have different views, it is more likely to be what *you* want that gets respected.

One way to make it easier for yourself is to use an online planning platform. If you set up an account on joincake.com for example, then you can store a lot of information there, including passwords

Section 7: Planning your perfect death…Writing your End-of-Life Plan

and PIN numbers with clear directions on who will get access to what in the event of your death.

You own this process. Your death is up to you. At least some aspects of it. Making your choices is empowering and putting it down on paper in a clear way can reduce some of the anxiety we feel around the idea of our own death.

You might even find, as I did, and some of my students have, that the whole process is very clarifying and life affirming. I created such a beautiful environment in my head, of my death scene, that I was reluctant to stop imagining it and return to my current life. It gave me pause for thought – if this was how I wanted to die, it must be things I hold dear. So why wasn't I living like that?

From there I started a two-year process of changing my way of life to align with those things that I now realised were most important to me. That included resigning from paid and voluntary jobs, decluttering massively, travelling more, meditating more, practicing yoga more, learning new skills and rebuilding my behaviours, habits, and attitudes more consciously. Studying death changed my life. I sincerely hope that if you discover any discrepancies, that discovery gives you a sense of direction to make whatever adjustments you can during the living part of your life too.

Section 8: My Shamanic experiences

Introduction

For many of you this might be the most confronting part of this book. Or the part that you can dismiss the most easily. I would have felt much like that too before I got involved in these activities. But several years of first-hand experience has convinced me that something is going on beyond the visible and tangible.

If the word soul or spirit is uncomfortable for you, these tales can as well be read considering these descriptions as energy. We know that energy can be invisible – any time someone has walked into the room, and you immediately feel they are upset or dangerous or full of joy, you have experienced that monitoring we do of each other's energy. This is very similar.

In this section I will share some of my stories with you. With deep respect for all the souls involved and gratitude to them, and to my own spirit guides and teachers for supporting me in this work. I feel there is much to be done in this area as we go through this unusual stage in human evolution where so much that was hidden is becoming seen.

There is an appetite in the air these days for uncovering wrongdoing and healing past traumas; releasing trapped or stuck souls can play an important part in that clearing process. Around the world, people with training in this area (known as psychopomp) are working to try to clear some of the backlog of tormented, traumatised, confused, stuck, or just lost souls. As soon as I start to do this work, they flock in, there is a desire to move on.

Soul releasing ceremonies

I have been doing this work for several years now with a wide range of clients. Some of whom are very much alive but interested in regathering themselves and the lost parts of their soul to have a better life and ultimately death. Others who are facing death and looking for support in their preparation for that journey, and others who have already died and either have come forward themselves for healing or via their friends and family or others affected by their unresolved spiritual state.

These examples show some of the different ways this can pan out. They are based on situations I have encountered first hand, though I have changed some details to protect the privacy of those involved. With respect and appreciation for all those who have been part of my learning on this fascinating journey into other realms.

A peaceful passing

Tom had died of heart failure in his early 70s. Not an unusual death but the suddenness was a shock to his friends and family. And possibly to his soul too. His sister contacted me to ask if I could carry out a soul release ceremony to check he was ok and transitioning as he wished.

Although in this case Tom's physical body was in a different country, and his death had been a few days earlier, the procedure I follow is the same as if I was at the bedside at the time of death.

When I don't have the body in front of me, I lay out a cloth and place crystals or flowers to mark the seven chakras – pinpointing the energy centres of the person. I also use representations of the four elements – earth, air, fire, and water – around the body.

I make sure I won't be disturbed and prepare firstly myself, and then the space where I will work. I make sure I have protected myself, since failing to do so can invite some of the wrong kind of energy into my own body. Using music and drumming I shift my state, so I am ready for the work.

My focus widens now to where I am working. Burning sage, incense or Palo Santo help cleanse the space and focus the energy. I check in with my spirit guides, and those of the space where I am working to see if they want to join in. I also ask if anybody wants to participate on behalf of Tom. Often a parent, grandparent or mentor will appear to support the process. Or the person's own spirit guides if they were in that space.

The last step before starting the procedure is the most important – asking Tom if *he* is willing to participate. I assure him that he will come to no harm and that this process is only to help him clear any energy from this life that he wishes to leave behind and support his transition to his next form of being. I mention that if he has any messages for loved ones then I will pass them on.

As has always been the case in my experience, Tom agrees to the ceremony, and I feel that he is now lying on the cloth in front of me. I welcome him into the space and settle in for our time together.

First, I conduct a general sweep of his energy body, working through his body using chanting and a rattle to check for any energy blocks or presence of negative energy that are presenting themselves to be rectified. I pay particular attention to the seven chakras which store emotional and spiritual information, as well as physical.

As I work through his body, I discover some issues that can be resolved to lighten his load as he moves on. It might help to imagine the energy body as a data file with everything from his life. I am looking for grievances, trauma, resentments, unprocessed emotions from events in his life. Sometimes the person may also be carrying events or feelings from their parents or grandparents – or even a past life.

Whenever I find such an issue, I work to gather more information. Is it unwanted energy left in his body? Or something missing? It may be manifesting as a feeling or a vision to me. Maybe I will see a weapon embedded in a leg or a representation of bad energy that could look like barbed wire or tar or a creature. I ask my spirit guides to show me the situation that generated this condition and they take me to a scene. I can usually deduce from clues – the surroundings, the way people are dressed, the situation that is taking place – a general idea of location and time in history. As the scene plays out in front of me it can become obvious if it is an energy memory from an ancestor or a past life. My own view is that it really doesn't matter how this energy has got stuck in someone's system, what matters is that they are ready to be free of it – which is where I may be able to help.

Often, I need to "rewind" the story to track back into causes. Why did someone's brother betray them in battle? What choices had the great grandmother made and why? In later examples I will share some of these more complex stories. In the case of Tom, there was energetic evidence of a head injury which turned out to be related to a past life event. By revisiting that event and bargaining with the person who inflicted harm I was able to change the story at that point – which released the energetic imprint of the event. Let it go. This releasing of unhelpful energy is considered key to a smooth passing. Learning the lessons arising from the incident can mean not having to repeat them in future lives.

Over time my experiences of this 'bargaining' has taken many forms. Some soldiers have been happy to change course for a few cigarettes. Other individuals require additional information or insight to see how their actions are not only harmful to the other person but also carry a toll for them, the inflictors of the damage. I have heard that some shamanic practitioners may fight rather than bargain, but this approach doesn't appeal to me in that realm any more than in this one.

I do find that those causing harm, usually have their own story of hurt or confusion too. They may have misunderstood a situation or reacted impulsively in the heat of the moment. Given the chance to change the course of history they are often more cooperative than one might expect.

In Tom's case, his injury had been during a torture session. His tormenter had thought Tom had important information, but he didn't. It was a misunderstanding. There was more to the story than this of course and some discussion was required to give the other man a clearer view of the situation and his best way forward, so he in turn could satisfy those to whom he was answerable.

In conclusion, I was able to resolve this past life injury and give Tom the chance to release it before moving on to his next stage. Other than this, Tom was happy and satisfied with his life and accepting of his death. He had some messages of support and love for his family, reminding them how much he would have hated a slower death or any kind of reduction of capacity. This near instant departure was what he would have chosen and, though sympathetic for their shock and grieving process given the suddenness, he didn't regret it and hoped they could come to see things the same way over time.

Soul shepherding

I was called to the site of Jose's death by suicide by the owners of the house he was renting. They wanted to make sure he had passed on or help him if he had not.

I entered the house with some trepidation. It was my first case of dealing with a suicide and I wasn't at all sure how things would be. The locals pointed out the house and showed me where to go but were uneasy about coming inside. Then the gardener offered to escort me to the room where Jose had ended his life. I opened the French windows wide, spread out my cloth and set the stage to see if he needed, and was open to, any help.

The gardener asked if he might stay, and sat opposite me, remaining silent and still throughout the ceremony. During my preparation of myself and the space before starting to work with Jose, I made sure to protect the gardener too.

There are many reasons why a soul can be "stuck" in this earthly realm. Suicide is often a violent and sudden end so there can be a degree of confusion. The soul may not have fully realised what has happened. Once I had Jose's permission to proceed with the ceremony this was one of the first things I checked. But in this case, he seemed to have thought carefully about the termination of his current life and was at peace with it.

However his spirit was still in the room and the scenes I was shown to explain this were all connected to his childhood, and particularly his relationship with his mother.

I travelled (energetically) to the land where she is living to understand things better. She was in deep grief of course, having recently received the news, and feeling terrible as any mother would in this situation, that her son had died in despair so far away. I comforted her and then had the challenge to convince her to let go. She had been holding part of her son's soul since he had left their homeland several years previously. There had been strife in the family and harsh words exchanged on all sides. She had found it very hard to accept his choice to just walk away and create a new life for himself on the other side of the world.

Now that his departure was final, she was clinging desperately to his soul part – what she considered to be the only part of him she still had.

As we learn in shamanic practice, this tendency to demand or offer or receive parts of another's soul is unhealthy for both parties. It is almost encouraged in the sentimental language of the West – look at the kind of phrases we hear in popular fiction and entertainment:

"I give you my heart."

"I am yours."

"You will always be a part of me."

These sound like fine sentiments, deep love and connection but in fact they interfere with our sovereignty, our wholeness. Imagine if instead we gave someone a physical body part – a hand say, or our literal heart – the act would seem gross, unnecessary, and potentially fatal. Giving away a part of our soul, our spirit body – or having it taken from us in an act of violence – is less obviously dangerous but has consequences just the same.

So an important part of the rituals we carry out for someone who is passing – and for those still living who wish to address such matters – is to check that they can gather most of their soul back together and release any soul parts belonging to somebody else they may have ended up.

In the case of Jose's mother, I had first to explain to her how hard it would be for her to grieve her son if she didn't relinquish this part of him. That she was holding him back and needed to remember – as in the words of the song, if you love someone, you set them free.

After this release, and some healing of other past traumas, I sensed Jose's energy body start to lift off the cloth. I carried out the final cleaning of chakras to minimise carryover into the next stage of his soul journey, and finally the unwinding motion that allows the energy body to leave this dimension. As I felt him surge away, I looked up at the gardener who had been sitting silently and immobile during the whole ceremony. He nodded and spoke for the first time.

"He is gone now."

I smiled in agreement and after a few moments silence I gathered up the flowers that had been in place of Jose's chakras so that I could take them down to the river and release them to the sea.

Letting go

I was asked by a friend if I could help her sick mother have a peaceful death. As mentioned, when I was talking about euthanasia, End-of-Life Doulas cannot play any role in illegal activities, but often a conversation is enough to help someone ease out of life. Other times – such as this – the person may be dying hundreds of miles away, or speak a different language, and a different approach is needed.

With her daughter participating remotely, I laid out my cloth and prepared for the ceremony. The dying woman was at the natural end of her life and had been ill for some time. Medical staff were surprised that she was still hanging on. In some cases, this can be because a mother feels she is not "allowed" to die – that her children need her. But this time even though her sons and daughters had all spoken to her and given their permission for her to leave, something seemed to be standing in her way.

As I proceeded through the body scan, the scene that emerged was from her early childhood. As a young girl 3 or 4 years old, she was being chased and bullied by a small group of boys in her village. Teasing and taunting her they frightened the child. But she was wriggly and quick, and she managed to slip out from between them and run – it felt like for her life – to the nearest house.

> "You're a bad girl. You'll go to hell for this when you die"
> they shouted after her.

She was scared and confused but she took in the idea that she had done something terribly wrong – without understanding what it might be. And at such a young age, that idea had lodged in her consciousness and plagued her throughout her life. When she had her own children, she was sure she would be a 'bad mother' since she was a 'bad girl'. So she had been distant and cold with them, trying to keep them from getting attached so she couldn't damage them.

Her life had been hard with this outlook and view of herself, and now her death was proving to be harder. What was she going to face on the other side? What terrible judgments and punishments awaited her? She was afraid all her life of living and now she was also afraid of dying.

In different times or cultures she might have been able to address this during her life, but that had not been available to her. However, it's never too late to set the record straight, and I was able to do some releasing work with her to amend the scene, ease her fear and give her some peace. She passed away an hour or two afterwards.

Healing past traumas

Sometimes I am asked to attend places where souls seem to have been stuck for a long time.

I was called to the small guesthouse by one of the residents. Like the other young women staying there, she always felt extremely uncomfortable in the shared kitchen, feeling an unwelcome and slightly threatening presence, a sense of being touched.

The young woman who had contacted me felt that this presence also stayed with her sometimes when she went back to her room, and she was finding it hard to relax or sleep. She asked me if I could investigate.

Indeed when I went into their shared kitchen, I could feel some troubled energy. I asked it if it was interested in working with us to find a better resolution for everybody and it agreed.

Returning to her room I had her lay down on the cloth and set up as usual. After my preparations I felt the need to scan her body and discovered that the presence had taken up residence in her spleen.

He said his name was Carl and he explained that he had been drawn to my client's youth and beauty because of his broken heart. He was in a lot of anguish.

I gently reminded him that he couldn't just invade her space like this, but he seemed inconsolable. Changing tack I asked him about his broken heart.

When I asked him his story, he shared a tragic tale. He had visited Bali – a much less common event than nowadays – and fallen deeply in love with a local girl, let's call her Ketut. But when she told her father, he went crazy and forbade the tryst. Ketut was devastated. She didn't want to disobey her father, but nor did she want to lose the love of her life.

Drawing my attention to the waterfall outside her window, he explained that the love of his life had plunged to her death there. He had never been able to leave this spot, feeling that he had to stay near the waterfall, and therefore near her. He had died a long time ago, but his spirit had stayed, wishing things had ended differently and full of guilt at being the unwitting cause of Ketut's death.

Clearly there was more of a story to be explored. I moved my attention to the girl who had thrown herself to her death at the waterfall. Ketut was a local girl and she shared that her father couldn't bear the idea that she had fallen in love with a white man who was visiting the area. He had forbidden her to meet with the man and she couldn't bear the idea of life without him. She hated being put in this position of having to choose between her father and her lover and chose this tragic course of action instead.

I backtracked further in time to try to understand her father's views and see why this was such an important issue for him.

> "She just doesn't understand how hard it was for me. I worked my whole life to be accepted by my village and she risked everything. My reputation would have been ruined. Of course, I never expected to lose her like that. I'd do anything to change how things turned out."

Time and space are not relevant in this work, so I sat with Ketut's grief-stricken father, just after his daughter's suicide. Why had he been so upset at the thought of her having a Western husband? He explained that he had grown up in circumstances of great shame and spent his whole life trying to earn the respect of his community. He just couldn't bear the thought of risking all that if they judged his daughter as turning her back on her culture.

More time travel then, to understand the source of his shame. His mother, Ketut's grandmother, had been born with shamanic powers, but they were not understood or encouraged by her family, who were worried the tendency might compromise her ability to find a husband. So she repressed her abilities.

I was shown the scene of her cooking, using a large knife to chop vegetables in preparation for the evening meal. The traditional cooking space was dark, and she was tormented by visions. Hearing a noise behind her she whirled round to see a large cobra reared up in the doorway. Frightened for her life, she panicked and lashed out with the machete, swiping at the beast just below its head. As she stepped back from the fatal blow, panting from the exertion, her eyes cleared and she realised it had not been a cobra at all, but her own husband.

As well as dealing with the tragedy of being widowed she also had to cope with the eternal shame of killing her own husband. The death was ruled accidental, and her husband's family continued to allow her and her son to live with them, but they were never allowed to forget what had happened.

Now I realised why the girlfriend who had died by throwing herself over the waterfall had been subjected to such a strong reaction from her father. His whole life had been overshadowed by his mother's act and he felt it had taken everything he had to earn back the respect of his community. He couldn't bear to see it put in jeopardy.

Maybe something could be done to avoid the incident in the first place? Why had his mother had this vision? I backtracked further into her life, discovering that she had frequently seen things in other ways as a child. Her family had been alarmed and embarrassed by her tendency to see people as animals or other kinds of creatures. Was she seeing some inner truth or just causing trouble? She was strongly deterred from voicing what she saw in case it jeopardised her chances of finding a husband, and over the years she had pushed it deep down inside her.

I was shown a new scene. This same young woman was on her way back from market. Trudging along the dusty road she passed a donkey, out alone. This felt like a possible moment of intervention, and I suggested to the young woman that she stop to stroke its nose. She was only partially surprised when the donkey spoke to her, asking if it could help her learn how to manage her special skills.

She was again only a little surprised when, upon agreeing, she saw the donkey shift into the shape of an old woman. The wise elder had seen the gifts of the young woman, and the struggles she was having living with them. She took her under her wing and spent many months teaching her how to work with these unusual abilities so that they did not need to be suppressed – or burst out of her in appropriate ways.

As the story rolled forwards – at much higher speed this time, I saw her marry and live a long and happy life with her husband and son.

Her son in turn found his own life partner and they were delighted with their beautiful daughter. When she fell in love with a foreigner visiting their country to study the plants in the area, they had to make some adjustments, but in time they came to love their son-in-law with his very different views of the world. Over games of cards he would have long conversations with his father-in-law, comparing different approaches in their two cultures to subjects as wide ranging as living with nature, managing disease, and dealing with unrest between neighbours.

I brought myself back into the room where I was working. I felt as though I had been gone for a very long time, but that is a common phenomenon – like dreams, these visions operate beyond our everyday understanding of time and space.

I checked my client's body again. It was clear. Her 'visitor' was no longer in residence. Looking up at the waterfall I smiled, its energy felt a little different. And neither my client nor the other girls staying in the hostel had any more trouble in the shared kitchen.

Healing space by completing passings on

As you will have seen in the last example, there can be some overlap between helping individual people and healing spaces. In this example the family contacted me because of their discomfort in their new home.

They felt that strange things were happening – accidents and mishaps that were out of character with their children's usual behaviour. The adults thought they felt something too, but most of the events seemed to focus on the children – either when they were playing in the garden or in their bedrooms.

The family weren't afraid of the situation, but they did feel that there was something that needed to be resolved so called me in to investigate.

As the reports I had were of children, I took a slightly different approach to usual, and spread out some picnic cloths on the grass in the garden. The family and their children went out so I could work uninterrupted. After my initial preparations and permissions, I started to sing some children's songs and then tell a story, just like I would if I was amusing a group of living children. One by one they started to emerge from their hiding places and move – some boldly, some shyly, towards where I was sitting.

There were 5 children in total, and two mothers. We played together for a while, building trust between us, then I started to talk to the children one by one. Their stories varied. One had died with her mother, during a difficult birth. Another pair were from a botched back street abortion. That accounted for the two women who were present. The other children had died in infancy. In each case there were some unresolved issues with the death which had caused them to get "stuck" around this piece of land.

The children had been delighted when the family who contacted me had moved into the house. Now there were toys to play with, other children to get to know. They had been attracted to this new energy from the surrounding area. Some of the incidents I'd been told about started to make sense. One little boy with a keen sense of mischief proudly admitted some of his actions.

I invited him to be the first to go on this new adventure. I explained to them all that they were ready now for the next step. That by flying off to another level they might have the opportunity to be born again, as real children. And that they would be going to a safe and lovely place.

The first boy lay down on the cloth I had prepared. I cleared some negative energy from his body – working with children is often a lighter experience than adults with their lifetime of experiences and decisions. Though of course even babies may be carrying ancestral or past life trauma.

When he was ready, I invited him to leave through the gap in the hedge in the corner of the garden. The others gasped as they saw his energy body lift away from the cloth and fly off.

One by one I worked with each child and then the two women. Each one was different, each had different energetic woundings and required different healings. But in the end the process was complete. I energetically sealed the gap in the hedge to protect the children currently living in the house from more unexpected visitors.

Healing the home by helping others

Long before I had got involved in this kind of work myself, I had personal experience of the unseen energies in a house.

I had moved into this home with my two young children. It did have an odd atmosphere, but served our needs and I pushed aside any sense of "not rightness".

Then I became pregnant with my third child and the tension in the house seemed to increase. A window cracked, a drain got blocked, the boiler broke down. I noticed that although it was a three-storey house, all the things going wrong were on a vertical plane cutting diagonally through the house.

Again I dismissed it as no more than an intriguing coincidence. My baby was born in the house and, as a typical third child, she was easy going and generally happy. Every now and then though, she would suddenly stare into the space in front of her and let out a scream. She would be inconsolable for a couple of minutes and then it would pass. It seemed inconsistent with her general character.

When I came down to the kitchen one morning to find the bread machine on the floor (it had been plugged in and 30 centimetres back from the edge of the countertop) I did some research on paranormal activity.

My research encouraged me to try to connect with whatever the unhappy energy was about, suggesting that it could be a cry for help. Over time I concluded that there had been a woman who died in childbirth in my bedroom, along with her baby. This pair had not passed on and they were increasingly upset by the successful pregnancy, birth and baby now present in the very space where they had met their end.

I called in an expert to help deal with the situation. At the end of his investigation we sat on a sofa at one end of the main room.

"I'm not convinced there's anything going on here,"

He was interrupted by a crash as the wastepaper basket ten metres away from us was flung over, spilling its contents across the floor.

"Ah. Well maybe I'm wrong,"

He went back to work and found a force field running diagonally across the house. Yes, in the same plane as where things went wrong across all three floors of the building.

He showed me a procedure, telling me I would know the right time to do it, to allow them both to move on and continue their soul journey.

All of this took some time, and my daughter was walking and starting to talk by the time I carried out the ceremony. I was alone and it only took a few moments. As soon as I'd finished, she appeared from the kitchen.

"Oh! Baby gone! Good" she said as soon as she waddled into the room.

After that I was a lot more convinced not only of life beyond the here and now, but also of my ability – and my daughter's – to sense it and to make helpful interventions where required and welcomed by all those involved.

Healing traumatised spaces

In some cases the energy story can be much more complex.

Visiting sites of multiple trauma - such as the Killing Fields in Cambodia which I experienced a few months ago – offers so many opportunities for helping souls progress that it is hard to know where to start.

But start one must.

I reminded myself of my visits to Ethiopia during the famine years. Or the project time I spent in Syrian Refugee Camps. It is very easy to feel overwhelmed in the face of this scale of human suffering, which is, for most of us, mercifully beyond our ken. In these situations I think the only way forward is to focus on whether you can be of service to anyone. If more than zero people might end up better off then that's something to hold onto.

So at the Genocide Museum in Cambodia I made a small start. 30 or so souls, from the children who had been killed on that site, came forward for help with passing and I supported each of those. Given that estimates suggest that up to two million may have been killed during the Khmer Rouge / Pol Pot era (1975-1979) then this is indeed a very small start. But imagine that one of those thirty souls was your child. Then it would be a good enough result.

And this is by no means the only place in the world that has endured extensive suffering. In a recent drive across the Somme, scene of that battle during the First World War (July 1 -November 18, 1916) that generated an estimated 950,000 German and British casualties, I could feel the weight of unprocessed souls. And what of Hiroshima or any other major scene of warfare or natural disaster?

It feels to me that all these places require that the souls still stuck there are supported in their journey. This is a critical part of healing both the space and those affected by the tragedy, so that we can move on, as humanity, and hopefully learn something from properly confronting these events on a one-by-one human scale.

Managing the scale

If we consider this Cambodia situation, plus all the natural disasters that have taken place in the world, plus all the individual acts of violence and unexpected abrupt deaths, then it is plausible that there is a huge backlog of souls waiting to find peace.

After my first round of training to become an End-of-Life Doula, I walked across our local park on my regular nightly dog walk. It was deserted as usual, only the bats and birds for company. But then suddenly I realised that the whole field was teeming with people. Mostly dressed differently to modern day. It wasn't frightening, but it was certainly a shock to realise how many entities there were – if we just tune in and allow them to be seen.

And I notice more and more often these days that when I'm doing a healing session for someone, then many other souls who have had similar experiences show up. This has happened when healing around a lost child for instance, or a death where there were still unresolved tensions. It's like a signal goes up alerting any souls in the vicinity that a train is about to leave, and they are welcome to get on it. Sometimes it is a handful of people, other times it has been hundreds.

Given this vast number of souls seeking assistance, then how can any of us working in this area manage the demand without finishing ourselves off from pure exhaustion?

Again it is like the famine situation or the refugee camps. First, we must come to terms with our own limitations. We cannot "fix" everything alone. We are here to do what we can do, not to do everything.

Having accepted that we need to see what would be a *sustainable* contribution that we could make. If you already have a busy job, young children to look after and a sick parent then be realistic. One of the advantages of this work is it doesn't require time or location in the way most caring roles do. For example, there might be an opportunity where you can support a good number of souls in a few minutes.

When considering what you could give to this soul support work, please also remember the importance of self-care. I might just spend an hour with a client, but I spend at least 30 minutes before in preparation and 1-2 hours afterwards, restoring my own balance.

One interesting approach to create some boundaries around the work, that I learnt during psychopomp training is the idea of a **Soul Hotel**.

The idea of this is that being available 24/7 is not manageable for most of us. We have other things to do and limited resources of health, time, patience or capacity to do this work. Yet the fact that we can do it means that we will often attract souls looking for that kind of support. My teacher described it as them being "drawn to the light".

The Soul Hotel is a rock crystal that you keep nearby – mine is on my bedside table. The souls that are attracted to you are also drawn to the rock crystal and can stay there, until the time and place when you choose to work with them. A time and place that is right for you. Some of them may have been waiting hundreds of years for resolution, and they are in another dimension anyway, so a few more earth days of waiting isn't going to make a significant difference to them.

Then when you are ready – at the Full Moon maybe – go to a suitable spot and release the souls one by one, helping them on their way.

Using this approach you might find you are supporting a dozen souls each full moon. Maybe more, maybe fewer. There is no need to worry about the numbers, just know that you are helping. And even if you only helped one person that would be a worthwhile contribution.

This energy dimension to death is a fascinating area and there are many ways you can deepen your understanding about it should you be so inclined. Courses such as the ones I did with the Sacred Trust or other organisations closer to your home are a safer way to get to know this world than exploring on your own. It is important to be properly protected and understand what you are dealing with. This is not casual work and things can go wrong. That said, with the right training and support it is also beautiful work that can greatly enrich your life.

Section 9: Meditations

Guided meditations can be a beautiful way to spend time with someone who is dying. I have included a few of my favourites here, and you can also find them on my YouTube channel if you prefer to listen. Some of them are better for relaxing the person you are working with – and you may find that as the carer you also feel more relaxed by calmly and slowly reading one of these meditations to them.

Others are more challenging and help us learn something about the dying process for ourselves.

Meditating is a way to open our hearts and share some possible empathy with another person. See if you can use it to develop some sense of how someone else might feel.

Meditation – Encountering Death

With thanks to Joan Halifax / Patricia Shelton / Richard Bosler who have developed and evolved this meditation.

A simplified version of a body scan, with shared breathing and then a guided meditation.

Start by making sure the dying person is comfortable and that you will not be disturbed. Depending on the condition of the dying person, you may need a third person to take care of any of their reactions so you can focus on creating an atmosphere of trust and leading the meditation.

The practice is calibrated to the needs and situation of the dying person. The light should be low, and the dying person covered up so that he or she is comfortable.

The caregiver starts by guiding the dying person through a simple version of a body scan beginning with the head. The practice can be done lying down, sitting on a practice cushion, or sitting on a chair. The person guiding the meditation then reads the following words.

This is a way we can meditate together.

It will involve a time for relaxation and a guided visualisation. I hope you will feel able to let go and be helped by what we are doing.

Start by letting your body relax and soften. Bring your attention to your breath. Breathe deeply into your belly.

Feel your whole body beginning to settle into the earth.

Breathing deeply, bring your awareness to the top part of your head, to your skull and scalp. Breathe into your scalp.

As thoughts arise just let them be.

Be aware of any tension in your scalp. On your next inhalation give space to whatever you experience.

Move your attention to your forehead. Be aware of your forehead, accepting whatever tension might be there.

Breathe into your temples. Accept any tension or pain in your temples. As you breathe out accept whatever you are experiencing.

If you can, put your hand over your eyes, as you breathe into them. Be aware of how your eyes feel. See if you can soften your eyes as you breathe in. As you breathe out, let go of all tension in and around your eyes.

Breathe in through your nose. Feel the air passing in and out of your nostrils. On your next inhalation bring your awareness to the feeling of cool air entering. Then feel the exhalation, passing out of your nostrils.

Gently move your awareness to your throat and neck. Breathe into this area, accepting whatever tension and tightness you might feel. As you exhale, rest lightly with your experience. Shift your awareness.

As you breathe into your shoulders, be aware of any sense of heaviness. On your in-breath, give your shoulders space. On your out-breath, drop them down easily towards the earth.

Let your awareness be in your arms. Inhaling and exhaling into them. How do they feel? Be aware of any tightness. There is nothing that you need to hold on to.

Touch your hands with your awareness. Let them open, palms facing upward. Breathe into the palms of your hands.

Your awareness is now in your spine. Breathe into your spine, letting it stretch with your in-breath, aware of your rib cage expanding. As you exhale, feel your spine lengthen.

Bring your attention to your chest and lungs. Breathe as deeply into your lungs as you are able and fill them so that your belly rises and gives your chest space in which to breathe deeply. Breathing in, feel your chest opening, your lungs expanding. Be aware of any tightness and any feelings of loss and sorrow. This is a very deep breath.

Now breathe into your heart. Be aware of openness or tightness in and around your heart. Soften around your heart.

Bring your attention to your diaphragm. Does your diaphragm yield as you breathe in? Inhaling deeply, feel your diaphragm giving your heart and lungs space in which to expand.

Be aware of your whole torso. As you exhale, bring your attention to your stomach. As you inhale, feel your guts expanding with the in-breath. On your out-breath be aware of any tension in your digestive system and let it go.

Be aware of the function of elimination performed by your bowels and bladder.

Then breathing in, appreciate your reproductive organs. Exhaling, give the entire pelvic area a feeling of space and ease.

Be aware of your legs and knees. Breathe into your thighs as you settle your attention into them. Breathing out, let your thighs soften.

On your inhalation feel gratitude for the support of your legs. Breathing out, appreciate your legs which have taken you so far in life.

Breathe into your knees. On the out-breath be aware of the small muscles around your knees. Breathe in healing to them and breathe out any tension and pain.

Breathe into your feet, bringing all your attention to your feet. On your out-breath, be aware of any tension. Imagine on your in-breath that you are breathing all the way through your body into your feet.

To complete this practice, slowly and smoothly bring your awareness gradually through your body.

Starting from your feet, move to your legs, to your stomach and pelvic area, to your chest, heart and lungs, to your spine, to your shoulders, arms and hands, to your neck, to your face, to the top of your head.

Breathe in and out smoothly as your awareness travels up and through your body.

When you have reached the top of your head return your awareness to your breath then let it gently spread to your whole body.

Stay this way for some minutes.

Take a few moments to relax with an open and quiet mind.

I will be silent now for a moment or two while I breathe with you. If you want to join me with the "ah" sound on the exhale, please do.

Now start to breathe gently and quietly in sync with the dying person. When you feel it is an appropriate time, breathe quietly and audibly the syllable "ah" on the out-breath of the dying person. Do this for 5-10 minutes so the one who is dying can really bring their attention to the out-breath. The sound should be soft almost like a yawn, the feeling is of surrender of letting go.

When the dying person is deeply relaxed, take a minute to read the prayer and visualisation from this next section or create something of your own with the person you are working with in mind.

Prayer

May I accept my anger, fear and sadness knowing that my heart is not limited by these feelings.

May all those I leave behind be safe and peaceful.

May I remember my consciousness is much vaster than this body.

As I let go of this body may I be open to the unknown.

As I leave behind the known may I live and die in ease.

Visualisation

Visualise a boundless ocean of light. As you breathe in the light, feel it fill your body.

Imagine that the boundaries of your body are merging with the light. Feel the light fill your heart, your lungs, your brain.

Feel your connection with the boundlessness of the light as it stretches out to the edges of the universe.

Abide in the light.

You are the light. The light is you.

Buddhist Five Elements Meditation

This meditation is about the dying process… the gradual release of each of these elements in our body. It can seem too harsh to us, as fully living people to ask someone to do this meditation. It is also valuable to us as we go on our journey of developing a more open and balanced relationship with death. It gives us a window into the experience of the person who is gradually leaving their body.

Ask the dying person, if they can, to adopt the 'Sleeping Lion' position. That is lying on their right side, legs comfortably bent, left arm along the body and right cheek resting on the right hand. If they feel comfortable, they can also use the little finger of their right hand to block the right nostril.

In this position, the yang energy of the right side of the body is held and calmed while the focus is on the yin energy on the left side of the body.

I invite you to imagine a supportive image (eg Christ, Buddha, Kwan Yin…) above the crown of your head. Any being who represents for you, the essence of awakening, compassion, love and essential goodness.

Your hope is that at your death, your consciousness will leave through the top of your head and manifest as the essence of enlightenment.

Let the breath become even and then focus your attention on your breath. Whatever comes up - resistance or concern, grief or joy, boredom, or story - notice and accept it and then return gently to the breath.

Imagine that this is an actual description of dying, of your dying. Notice what goes on for you as you do this practice. Let each of the feelings and sensations that come up for you, pass through your mind and body, be noticed, and then be released.

The dissolution of earth into water and the unbinding of the body

Imagine that you are in your bed at home. Friends and family are around you, but you are barely aware of them. You are somewhat agitated, and you accept this state of mind.

Your body is weak, you do not have the energy to do anything but simply be there. You are letting go.

As you die, feel your body becoming heavy, pressed down by a great weight. This heaviness is dense and deep, in the core of your body now.

Your body feels as if it is dissolving. Your legs and arms don't feel as if they belong to your body. You feel as though you are slowly sinking in water and a deep weariness penetrates every cell of your body. This body is letting go.

Your senses are less attuned to the outside world. Your sight is dim. It is difficult to open and close your eyes.

Your sensory grasp on the world is loosening as your body starts to slip away.

The outside world is slipping away from you as well. Your skin is pale as your blood pressure drops. The blood withdraws into the central part of your body.

You are drowsy and weak, with no interest in the outside world. You sink deeper and deeper into a blurry vague mental state. Whatever visions you see appear like blue mirages.

This is the dissolution of the body and of our relationship to the physical world. These feelings of heaviness, drowsiness, being weighed down, the loss of definition. This withdrawing of colour from our bodies. The loss of control and the ability to see the physical world around us.

In this state of mind and body, be awake and effortlessly present.

The mind can be still and reflective as you let go. Be present as this body is dying. This body is not you.

This is the dissolution of the element of earth as it sinks into water and this form unbinds into feelings.

The dissolution of the water element into fire and the unbinding of feelings

Feel your body dissolve as you let go. Your hearing is diminished, and you sink into a blurred state of mind. Your nose is running, saliva is leaking out of your mouth, there is a watery discharge coming out of your eyes.

It is difficult to hold your own. Your skin is clammy as fluids leave the body. The body becomes parched. Your skin is papery, your mouth is dry, and your lips are chapped. Your tongue is thick, sticky and heavy. Your throat is scratchy and clogged. Your nostrils seem to cave in, burning with dryness as you inhale.

Your eyes feel sandy and sting.

You are not passing much urine.

You have a thirst that no amount of water can quench.

Let go fully into the dryness. Release the fluid element of your body of water. Your mind feels hazy, and you are irritable. You have ceased to experience pain, pleasure or even indifference. You do not differentiate between physical and mental impressions - those kinds of distinctions are not important to you now.

When you look behind your eyes you see a vision of swirling smoke.

The water element is dissolving into fire.

This is the end of your responsiveness to phenomena as you must go. Wake up in this vision of swirling smoke.

The dissolution of the fire element into air and the unbinding of perceptions

As the fire element of your body begins to dissolve into air, your body feels cool.

Heat withdraws from your feet and hands into the body's core. Your breath is cold as it passes through your mouth and nose.

Your mouth, nose and eyes dry out even more. Your ability to perceive is further diminished.

The fire element is dissolving into the element of air. You cannot smell anything. You are not hungry, nor can you digest food. You cannot drink or swallow.

The in-breath is less strong, and the out-breath is longer.

Your mental perception alternates between lucidity and confusion.

You cannot see, hear, taste, touch or smell as the sense fields fade away.

Your in-breath is short, your out-breath is long.

You cannot remember the names of your loved ones and you cannot recognise those around you.

You have lost any sense of purpose in your life and have no interest in what is going on around you.

You may feel as though you are being consumed in a blaze of fire that rises into space. Let go into this fire as your mind releases itself.

Or you may see sparks, almost like fireflies. Wake up in this vision of shimmering sparks.

This is the dissolution of the fire element into air and the unbinding of your ability to perceive.

The dissolution of the wind element into space and the unbinding of mental formations

You have now given up any sense of volition.

Accept this aimlessness, empty of meaning and purpose.

Your in-breath is short, your out-breath is long.

The mind is no longer aware of the outside world as the element of air dissolves.

You have visions. These visions relate to who you are and how you have lived your life. You may see your family or your ancestors in a peaceful setting. You may see beautiful people - saints or friends welcoming you. You may relive pleasant experiences from your past.

You may also have demonic visions. If you have hurt others those whom you have injured may appear to you. Difficult moments of your life may arise to haunt you. You may see people with whom you have had negative interactions attacking you. You may even cry out in fear.

Do not identify with these visions, simply let them be. The element of air is dissolving.

You do not have to do anything. Just practice this breath of release and let go of everything.

Your tongue is thick and heavy. Its root is blue. You have lost your taste for life as you lose the sense of taste.

You cannot feel texture or body sensations. Your body is barely moving. The last energy of your body is withdrawing to your body's core. Whatever heat is left in your body now resides around the heart.

The in-breath is short, a mere sip of air. The out-breath is long and uneven.

Your eyes, gazing into emptiness, roll upward. No intellect is present. Your consciousness at this point is reduced to a smaller and smaller entity.

After three more rounds of respiration, your body lifts slightly to meet the breath which does not enter.

Mental functions cease altogether. Consciousness dissolves into space. The perception from the outside is that you are dead. Breathing and brain function have stopped.

Know this empty state. Surrender to it.

This is the element of wind dissolving into space.

At the moment of physical death, you see a small flickering flame like a candle. It is suddenly extinguished, and you are without awareness.

The inner dissolutions

From the crown, a white drop is propelled by the inner winds downward through the central channel toward the heart. This is the male essence. And anger transforms into profound clarity.

You experience an immaculate autumn sky, filled with brilliant sunlight.

A red drop from the base of the spine is propelled upward through the central channel towards the heart. This is the female essence. and desire transforms into profound bliss.

You experience a vast and clear, copper red autumn sky of dusk.

The white and red drops meet in the heart and surround your consciousness.

The winds enter your consciousness. You are now freed from the conceptual mind.

Darkness like a deep autumn night sky appears as you dissolve into unconsciousness.

Out of this nothingness you are one with the clear dawn sky. Free of sunlight, moonlight and darkness.

You are bliss and clarity now. The clear light of presence is liberated. The mother of your awareness. This is your ultimate great perfection. This is the actual moment of death.

Yoga Nidra for Chronic Pain

You may be familiar with Yoga Nidra – a very specific form of yoga where participants simply lie in savasana (on their back with legs apart and arms by their sides) and listen to the words, letting them wash over them and trying to release any other thoughts. This can be a soothing meditation for someone who is in a lot of pain. It may be hard for them to focus at first, but a soothing voice and gentle rhythm of the yoga nidra might take them to a different place.

Begin by lying on your back with your feet slightly wider than hip-width apart. Place a small pillow or thinly folded blanket under your head to keep your forehead level or just slightly higher than your chin. You can also place folded blankets or a bolster under your knees for extra support.

First, come into the present moment. Focusing on the here and now, notice any sounds you hear. Then bring your awareness to your body, noticing the touch of the air on your skin, how your clothes feel against your skin. Now transition from the outside world to the inside by focusing on inner sensations, and what it feels like. What are you experiencing in your body?

Next, allow yourself to be fully supported by the ground. The body is relaxed and at ease. You are being held by the earth rather than holding yourself. Scan your body for tension; see if you can allow this tension, even only a small percentage of it, to melt away. Allow this tension to release its grip in its own time.

Become aware of your breath without trying to direct it. Trust that you don't need to control your breathing, that it will occur naturally without your effort. Let the body and breath unite as you relax and witness their inherent connection, without getting involved. You are not the breather. You are the awareness of the body breathing.

Become stiller and quieter. Invite the mind to come to a single form of consciousness. Allow that form of awareness simply to believe:

I am practicing yoga nidra,
I am practicing yoga nidra,
I am practicing yoga nidra.

Let that be the form of your consciousness for the rest of the practice.

Become totally aware of your body, any sensations you feel, your energy level, and the quality of your mind. This is witness consciousness—a state of awareness from which you can observe the fluctuations of your body and mind.

Breathing continues effortlessly, with inhales melting into exhales, exhales transforming into inhales.

Senkalpa (intention)

Feel as if the heart herself is breathing. Evoke there in the heart a feeling of thankfulness. A sense of gladness simply for the opportunity to experience this relaxation. Feel this gladness as a gentle warmth that radiates from the heart.

Breathe into this warmth and be thankful for the opportunity to do this. As the mind enters the heart, hear the breath of the heart as if it were the voice of the heart's own wisdom.

Be open now to whatever wisdom may come through to you with the breath of the heart. Welcome it like a beautiful seed to plant in your heart. It is surely already growing and thriving.

Body scan

And now take your attention back to the physical body and prepare to guide the mind around the body as if the light of the mind's attention comes to shine on each part of the body in turn.

While the mind travels freely following the instructions, the physical body remains motionless taking deep breaths. See the light of the mind's attention in the form of bright little stars. As consciousness travels to each part of the body that I name, place a star on that part of the body leaving it to shine there.

It is as if the whole body begins as a dark night sky, and as the mind travels round it bringing bright starlight to each part, the body is illuminated like a great constellation of stars in the sky

First bring your awareness to the tip of the tongue and shine a bright star at that point. Then place stars on the floor of the mouth, the roof of the mouth, the upper teeth and gums, the lower teeth and gums, the inside of the right cheek, the inside of the left cheek.

Move your awareness to the inner part of your right ear and shine bright stars in and around the ear, the whole of the right ear.

Move your awareness to the inner part of the left ear and shine bright stars all the way through and round the inner left ear, the outer left ear. The whole of the left ear.

Feel both ears twinkling with the starlight of conscious awareness.

Shine a bright star on the back of the head and have a bright star twinkling on the crown, and another just above your head.

Then place a bright star on the right temple, left temple, forehead.

Right eye, left eye. Right eyebrow, left eyebrow, and between the eyebrows.

Right cheek, left cheek, then to the nose, right nostril, left nostril, bridge of the nose, tip of the nose.

Upper lip, lower lip, chin, jawline, whole head. Feel the whole head twinkling with tiny stars, the light of conscious awareness.

Move your awareness to your neck and throat. Shine a star on the right collar bone, left collarbone, and one in the place between the two.

Move the awareness to shine stars on your right shoulder and armpit, right upper arm, elbow, forearm, right wrist, back of right hand, palm of right hand. Right thumb, index finger, middle finger, ring finger, little finger. Be aware of the whole of the right-hand twinkling with the light of conscious awareness.

Move your attention up the right arm and across to the left shoulder, left armpit, upper arm, elbow, forearm, wrist, back of hand, palm, thumb, index finger, middle finger, ring finger, little finger. Be aware of the whole of the left-hand twinkling with the light of conscious awareness.

Starting in the centre of the chest, move your attention along the length of the breastbone, right ribs, left ribs, middle of right shoulder blade, left shoulder blade, between the two.

Place stars at the back of the waist, right waist, left waist, lower back, right pelvis, left pelvis, right buttock, left buttock, naval, pubic bone.

Now move your attention to place a star on the right groin, top of right thigh, back of thigh, right kneecap, calf, shin, ankle, heel. Place stars along the top of the right foot and one on each toe – first the big toe, then the 2nd, 3rd, 4th, 5th toes. The whole of the right foot and leg is now twinkling with tiny stars, the light of conscious awareness.

Next do the same starting at the left groin, top of left thigh, back of thigh, left kneecap, calf, shin, ankle, heel. Place stars along the top of the left foot, one on each toe – the big toe, 2nd, 3rd, 4th, 5th toes. The whole of the left foot and leg are now twinkling with tiny stars, the light of conscious awareness.

Be aware of the whole right side of the body. Be aware of the stars twinkling along the whole of the right side, the foot, leg, arm, hand, torso.

The whole of the right-side is twinkling with the stars of conscious awareness.

Be aware of the whole left side of the body. Be aware of the stars twinkling along the whole of the left side, foot, leg, arm, hand, torso. The whole of the left side is also twinkling with the stars of conscious awareness.

Bring the light of the mind's attention to shine now inside the body. Into the womb space, or the place where you would have a womb. Let the light here shine in the form of a little moon. A moon inside you. See the light of the inner moon shining. See all the little stars twinkling now in the constellation of the whole body.

Bring the light of mental awareness to the whole of the right arm and hand. left arm and hand. Now both arms and hands together

Now take the awareness to the whole of the right leg, foot, left leg, foot, both legs and feet together

Aware now of both arms and both legs together.

See the starlight twinkling through the whole of the right side. Whole of the left side. Both sides together.

See the starlight twinkling through the whole of the head and the moonlight shining in the pelvis and now be aware of the whole body like a constellation of bright shining stars. The whole of the body like the night sky twinkling with the light of conscious awareness.

Feel the whole of the left body resting on the floor remaining alert and attentive to the practice.

I am practicing yoga nidra.
I am practicing yoga nidra.
I am practicing yoga nidra.

Let that be the form of awareness.

Physical Pain

Know that these healing images are here for you to use whenever you feel your pain, whether it is physical, mental, or emotional.

Now visualize your chronic pain—as if it had a form. Everyone's pain will look different. It could be a very realistic, concrete object or a shapeless image representing more of a void, a vacuum, a black hole, an abyss. Once you get a firm mental image, fill it with your awareness without reacting or identifying with it.

Then imagine your pain's ultimate antidote. Conjure an image of a healing that can eradicate the image of your physical pain. Or if the image of your pain is less concrete, perhaps the healing image will create substance where there was none. Exist in the witness consciousness of the pure healing power of this image and allow it to remove every trace of the image of your pain.

Emotional Pain

Now think of a lack of ease—a "dis-ease" in your mental/emotional body. How does this feeling manifest? What does it look like? How does your body experience this mental sensation of dis-ease? Become aware of these details without reacting or identifying with any image, or absence of image, that arises.

Now prepare the antidote for this image and feeling - something different to what you imagined for your physical pain. Visualize the healing imagery and become aware of the associated sensations. Let the healing imagery be stronger than the mental feeling and visualize it sweeping the dis-ease away, over and over, using your awareness to give persistency and strength to this healing image.

Breathe into the imagery and let it soak into every layer of your mind and body. Let awareness exist in the process of healing and know that there is no success or failure, no right or wrong; there is merely abiding in the healing image you have created.

Return

Slowly come back to the body. Take some deep breaths to inspire movement in your fingers, toes, and limbs. Notice the body emerging from the heaviness. As you come back to a waking state, rest in the awareness that the antidote to your pain is always within you.

Know that these healing images are there for you to use whenever you feel your pain, whether it is physical, mental, or emotional.

Yoga nidra is a powerful practice that can invite a spacious state of awareness. I hope that, over time, this specific practice brings you a sense of peace, and perhaps some relief from chronic pain.

Yours in health and healing, namaste.

Grief meditation

This meditation is borrowed from death guru and Buddhist nun Joan Halifax following the Zen tradition. It reads like a prayer and the soothing rhythms can be a great comfort.

May I be open to the pain of grief.

May I find the inner resources to be present for my sorrow.

May I accept my sadness knowing I am not my sadness.

May I accept my anger, fear, anxiety and sorrow.

May I accept my grief, knowing that it does not make me bad or wrong.

May I forgive myself for not meeting my loved one's needs.

May I forgive myself for mistakes made and things left undone.

May I be open with myself and others about my experience of suffering and loss.

May I find peace and strength that I may use my resources to help others.

May all those who grieve be released from their sorrow.

Life and death are of supreme importance.

Time passes quickly and opportunity is lost.

Let us awaken. Awaken.

Do not squander your life.

Tong-len meditation

Tong-len is a very specific style of meditation that invites us to release pain and anxiety by feeling compassion for others experiencing the same thing. That can seem counter-intuitive, but I strongly recommend that you give it a go before dismissing the idea. My students have found it to be of great value.

Sit comfortably and settle in.

Let's begin with a mindfulness meditation, maintaining your focus on the breath. As you breathe in, be present with breathing in. As you breathe out, be present with breathing out. Acknowledge distracting thoughts and emotions as they arise, let go of them, and return to connecting with the breath. Now link your intention - to release your pain and suffering - to the breath.

On the exhale, breathe out the light of basic goodness: your wish to help alleviate all pain and suffering. On the inhale, invite the smoky darkness of negativity and suffering to enter your heart where it will be transformed into light.

Imagine that your initial object of compassion is a frightened stray dog cowering in a cage at an animal control facility. Begin the exchange by breathing in the darkness of her fear, isolation, and bewilderment so that she can be relieved of it.

As you breathe out, let your affectionate heart radiate soothing, gentle light beams that touch, reassure, and comfort her. She becomes confident and happy, cared-for and loved.

Extend your meditation to other scared dogs. Inhale their fear and confusion. Exhale love and peace so they all feel comforted. Now consider all caged animals. Inhale their fear and confusion. Exhale love and peace so they feel comforted.

Extend your awareness now to all beings that feel trapped. Breathe in the darkness of their distress, breathe out the light of freedom and peace; imagine their relief and allow it to touch your heart.

Expand the circle of goodwill to all beings everywhere. Breathe in suffering and negativity. Breathe out happiness and comfort. Allow your heart's natural goodness to shine unreservedly and touch the world with its grace.

Finally, relax into open meditation and sit within that for a few more minutes.

Section 10: In conclusion

We are now almost at the end of our journey together and I would like to cast an eye over some of the main themes we have explored. Starting with the subtitle of this book:

Reclaim dying. Embrace living.

Reclaim dying

For too long we have allowed others to tell us what dying should mean. Religious leaders, our families, so-called polite society, class-based systems, power-based systems, political systems. We don't have to live in countries that have been colonised to experience this colonisation of death. Anybody whose inner guidance has been quashed or belittled by the powers-that-be has experience of this.

We are moving into an era in history where we are opening our eyes to this experience in all walks of life. And following decolonising theory, we have some stages to go through. Realising and rediscovering our own intuition and belief systems, mourning what has been lost – accepting those past deaths we might do differently now, dreaming of what could be and then making a commitment to action to bring that dream about.

This book is part of my commitment to action. There is much more to be done.

Embrace living

There's no getting away from it, despite millennia of searching for the elixir of life, current science makes it likely we will all die. And even if, somehow, we don't, we will be touched by the deaths of other people around us.

Given that it is such a fundamentally affecting and inevitable part of life, then I believe it is worth spending some time facing it, getting to know it, and finding our own version of peace and empowerment within it.

Living our life backwards from the point of our death can bring a great sense of spaciousness and appreciation into our days. The literary technique known as *in media res*, where the death of a principal character is shared very early in the story, leaving the rest of the book to reveal the events leading up to it, can be used to diminish the sense of tragedy. We know the lead character will die so we can get used to that idea early on and focus instead on the story.

What if we lived like this? Knowing that we will one day die and therefore living life to the full, relishing every up and down, every sunset, every mouthful of food, every smile? Can you remember the first music track you bought and how much you loved it? How does that compare to the tenth? The hundredth? Having less of something doesn't necessarily mean less enjoyment.

We know from working with people with terminal illnesses that it doesn't cause them to be miserable for every moment left to them. There is still laughter during my sessions with the dying.

Radio producer Mel Dee Dzelde struggled with Stage 4 cancer for four years and then found she also had motor neuron disease.

Section 10: In conclusion…Reclaim dying. Embrace living.

Despite years of unwelcome test results and challenging treatments, she has this to say to us:

> *I'm so grateful to wake up each morning and to be blessed with another day in my joyous life. I literally give thanks each morning for the day.* (Dzelde, 2021)

We don't need to wait until death is looming very close to have these breakthroughs. We can start now. Embracing our dying, clarifying our ideas about our own deaths, and then enjoying the space that creates - to live life in the way that matters most to us. Ditch what you don't need – possessions, ideas, maybe acquaintances, responsibilities, unnecessary chores – so you can focus your life energy onto what really matters.

The dying have advice for us too…

Advice from the Dying to the Living

This list of the top five deathbed wishes was originally compiled by Bronnie Ware in an article which then went viral, encouraging her to create her book The Top Five Regrets of the Dying (Ware, 2019). Bronnie is an experienced palliative care worker, and her observations are an important reminder to all of us to live our life like we mean it.

To live a meaningful life, an intentional life, a joyful life. And to keep in check our human tendency to get distracted or spun into states by media, social media, friends, family, society… this is your life. Live it your way. And bear in mind these 5 regrets of the dying:

1. I wish I'd had the courage to live a life true to myself, not the life others expected of me.

Section 10: In conclusion…Reclaim dying. Embrace living.

2. I wish I didn't work so hard.

3. I wish I'd had the courage to express my feelings.

4. I wish I had stayed in touch with my friends.

5. I wish that I had let myself be happier.

I'm always particularly moved by the last one. What kind of society have we created where this is a problem? It is heart-breaking – but at least, if we aren't dying yet, we still have time to do something about it. What might you change about your living so that you feel better about your dying when it comes?

There is also much inspiration to be found in Rodney Smith's books. His background of meditation, monastic life and hospice experience has brought him to profound realisations about the nature of death and dying. Observing our increased interest in the topic, he also comments that we tend to keep it in our mind rather than take it into our hearts. He suggests:

> *"If we are to be altered by death, we must give it our full attention. This means reflecting on it and learning its lessons. When we allow ourselves to learn from death, the psychic distance between those who are dying and those who are healthy narrows."*
> *(Smith, 1997)*

Let us live consciously so we might die consciously.

Fare thee well

Finally, to repeat the words of Zen Hospice founder Frank Ostaseski's that I used at the start of this book:

Section 10: In conclusion…Reclaim dying. Embrace living.

*Let death guide you into living a more loving and
meaningful life.*

My intention with this book has been to share some of the journey
I have been on with death over the last few years, hoping that
these reflections might both challenge some of our societal fears
and avoidance of death, and give the arc of your life a more
gracious curve.

I wish you a joyful and expansive life, where its many lessons are
seen and welcomed, and its ending is a peaceful completion. And
however things turn out, I wish you a good relationship with both
your life and your death.

Section 11: Resources

Continuing your journey

There are a huge number of resources online, in books and in person, available to those who wish to go further on this journey. In fact an overwhelming amount, so although I am suggesting a few things here that I have found helpful (also see Bibliography at the end of this book), you will have to trust your intuition and be guided to what feels like it might be most useful for you. You can always stop reading or listening to something that doesn't resonate. I suggest that if you don't relate to something, you trust it might not be for you, or it might not be the best time for you to receive that information.

Maybe you are interested to find out more about being an End-of-Life Doula yourself or learning some of the shamanic practices I have talked about. Here are some pointers to get you started on the next stage of your journey with death.

End-of-Life Doula Training

* End-of-Life Doula training was only in person when I studied it, but the pandemic changed that. Now you can choose what works best for you. I studied with Living Well Dying Well in the UK (www.lwdwtraining.uk) (UK). There are others around the world. Like choosing a yoga teacher training or anything else in the multi-option world we live in, let yourself be guided to what feels right for you.

- Soul Midwife training (www.soulmidwives.co.uk) is a little different and focuses on the spiritual aspect of dying. It is also a shorter training which might work better for you.

- Think also what kind of journey you want to go on. For me, it worked well that my End-of-Life Doula training was so thorough, experiential, and over two years. I feel it took me that long to develop a depth of understanding and to reprogram so many of my old beliefs on the subject. You may already have relevant background or experience though and therefore feel that a shorter process is more appropriate for you.

Apps and Websites

- Conscious Dying (US) https://www.livingdying.org
- Meditation support in dying
  https://oshosammasati.org/death-dying-toolkit/
- https://www.theguardian.com/lifeandstyle/2012/sep/07/right-to-die-mother-nicklinson
- Digital legacy mgmt (photo, profiles, purchases)
  https://digitallegacyassociation.org
- https://www.joincake.com
- https://www.gathermycrew.org.au/
- https://jointlyapp.com/

Books

There are so many, but here are a few I personally have found helpful. Any of these people will also have freely available material on websites and YouTube.

- **Joan Halifax**: Buddhist nun with vast experience of accompanying people at death. *Being with Dying.*
- **Elisabeth Kübler-Ross**: MD, founder of hospice concept, 5 stages of grief. *Death and Dying*
- **Frank Ostaseski**: Buddhist teacher and cofounder of the Zen Hospice Project. *The Five Invitations*
- **Louise Hay and David Kessler**: founder of Hay House, *You can Heal Your Heart*
- **Sogyal Rinpoche:** *The Tibetan Book of Living and Dying*
- **Starhawk:** *The Pagan Book of Living and Dying*
- **Julia Samuel,** *Grief Works*
- **Liz Rothschild,** *Outside the Box* (also see YouTube)
- **Amanda Blainey** *Do Death for a life better lived*
- **Henry Marsh-** *Do no Harm* and *And Finally*
- **Tony Walters** (storytelling approach to grief) www.researchgate.net/publication/240532074_A_New_M odel_of_Grief_Bereavement_and_Biography
- SARK interview on succulent wild grief (YouTube)

Groups

- Dying Consciously (Facebook)
- Death Chat (Facebook)
- Grief Chat (Facebook)
- Coffin Club (Facebook)

- Death cafes
- Threshold Choirs sing around the bedside of the dying and exist in many countries (thresholdchoir.org).

Film/TV/Podcasts

- See my playlist on YouTube of the videos referenced in this book, and others: bit.ly/sacreddeathvideos
- Time of Death (documentary series, Amazon TV)
- The Father (film, struggling with aging and dying)
- The Way (film, losing a son)
- Pieces of a Woman (film, infant mortality)
- Aftersun (film, reconciling with loss of father)
- Bowel Babe Documentary - Deborah James
- Emma Clare on Talking with Cancer podcast.
- How to have life changing conversations about the end of life. Goodgrieffest.com

Bibliography

(n.d.). Retrieved from
https://en.wikipedia.org/wiki/Doreen_Lawrence

(2013). Retrieved from Radiolab.org:
https://radiolab.org/podcast/262588-bitter-end

(2022). Retrieved from Compassion and Choices:
https://www.compassionandchoices.org/our-issues/vsed

40 under 40. (n.d.). Retrieved from Fortune:
https://fortune.com/40-under-40/2020/suelin-chen/

Alexandros Katsiferis, S. B. (2023). *Sex differences in health care expenditures and mortality after spousal bereavement.* Retrieved from Plos One:
https://journals.plos.org/plosone/article?id=10.1371/journal.pone.0282892

Barry, E. (2022). Retrieved from Time Magazine:
https://time.com/6173229/countries-abortion-illegal-restrictions/

Bird, N. (2022). Retrieved from BBC News:
https://www.bbc.com/news/uk-wales-63599107

California, U. o. (2015, Aug 28). Retrieved from Science Daily:
https://www.sciencedaily.com/releases/2015/08/150828135219.htm#:~:text=The%20truth%20is%20more%20depressing,that%20%2D%2D%20around%2037%20percent.

Caludi. (n.d.). *The tribe that keep their dead relatives at home.* Retrieved from

Bibliography

https://www.escape.com.au/destinations/asia/the-tribe-that-keeps-their-dead-relatives-at-home/image-gallery/6b4fc89987417563bd9f9f128131ec28#:~:text=In%252525252520a%252525252520custom%252525252520that%252525252520many,a%252525252520year%252525252520for%2

Capacitar international. (n.d.). *What Capacitar teaches*. Retrieved from Capacitar International: https://capacitar.org/work/what-capacitar-teaches/

Damodharan Dinakaran, V. S. (2021). *Dengue and Psychiatry: Manifestations, Mechanisms, and Management Options.*

Death Penalty Demographics. (2023). Retrieved from Deathpenaltyinfo.org

Deathpenaltyinfo.org. (n.d.). Retrieved from https://deathpenaltyinfo.org/death-row/overview/demographics

Dr. Jasmine Shaikh, M. (2022, 3 28). Retrieved from Medicine Net: https://www.medicinenet.com/is_it_normal_to_be_scared_of_labor_and_delivery/article.htm

Dzelde, M. D. (2021). *Mamamia*. Retrieved from https://www.mamamia.com.au/author/mel-dee-dzelde/

Elliott., J. (n.d.). *Chief of the neuromuscular disorders section at the University of Texas Southwestern Medical Center*. NBC News.

Evans, D. (2016). Retrieved from Center for Disability Rights: https://cdrnys.org/blog/advocacy/as-a-film-fundamentals-is-just-okay-the-disability-community-could-do-better/

Gander, K. (2019). *Newsweek.*

Guttmacher.org. (2022, March). Retrieved from https://www.guttmacher.org/fact-sheet/induced-abortion-worldwide

Halifax, J. (n.d.). *A Buddhist Perspective on Grieving.* Retrieved from https://www.upaya.org/dox/Grief.pdf

Journal of Humanistic Psychology. (2019). *The Psychological Correlates of Decreased Death Anxiety After a Near-Death Experience.* Retrieved from Research Gate: https://www.researchgate.net/publication/337771633_The_Psychological_Correlates_of_Decreased_Death_Anxiety_After_a_Near-Death_Experience_The_Role_of_Self-Esteem_Mindfulness_and_Death_Representations

Kellie R. Hannan, F. T. (2022). Racial Sympathy and Support for Capital Punishment: A Case Study in Concept Transfer. *Deviant Behavior.*

Kelly M. Hoffman, S. T. (2016). *National Library of Medicine.* Retrieved from https://www.ncbi.nlm.nih.gov/pmc/articles/PMC4843483/

Kerr, C. (2020). *Death is but a Dream.* Buffalo.

Kessler, E. K.-R. (2014). *Life Lessons, Two Experts on Death and Dying Teach Us About the Mysteries of Life and Living.*

Lim, R. (2016). Retrieved from Awakening Birth: https://awakeningbirth.net/index.php/delayed-cord-clamping/

Bibliography

Mackenzie, S. (2012). Retrieved from The Guardian:
https://www.theguardian.com/lifeandstyle/2012/sep/07
/right-to-die-mother-nicklinson

Medicine, J. H. (2021, 8 8). Retrieved from Johns Hopkins
Medicine:
https://www.hopkinsmedicine.org/health/conditions-
and-diseases/staying-healthy-during-pregnancy/4-
common-pregnancy-complications

Mishara, B. &. (2016). *Understanding Suicide.* Retrieved from
https://www.understandsuicide.com/_files/ugd/2caebd_
62c53227c2784fd5ae5d3833321e7d62.pdf?index=true

Orlando, A. (2021). Retrieved from Discover Magazine:
https://www.discovermagazine.com/mind/what-a-
hospice-physician-who-interviewed-1-400-patients-can-
tell-us-about

Ostaseski, F. (2017). *The Five Invitations.* Bluebird Books for Life.

Prof Erica Borgstrom, K. B.-J. (2023). *End of Life Doula UK.* Open
Thanatoogy, The Open University.

Ross, E. K. (1969). *On Death and Dying.* Scribner.

Seber, C. (2017). *Cleaning the dead: the afterlife rituals of the Torajan
people.* Retrieved from theguardian.com:
https://www.theguardian.com/world/gallery/2017/oct/
13/cleaning-the-dead-the-afterlife-rituals-of-the-torajan-
people

Shofia Maharani Khoirun Nisa, I. Q. (2018). Retrieved from Journal
of Maternal and Child Health:
https://thejmch.com/index.php?journal=thejmch&page=a
rticle&op=view&path[]=79

Smith, R. (1997). *Lessons from the Dying*. Amazon.

Suzuki, S. (1970). *Zen Mind, Beginner's Mind*.

Tandon, R. (2021, June). *National Library of Medicine*. Retrieved from https://www.ncbi.nlm.nih.gov/pmc/articles/PMC8110323/

Tonkin, L. (1996). Growing around Grief. *Bereavement Care*. Retrieved from Bereavement Care.

Villoldo, A. (2018). Retrieved from The Four Winds: https://thefourwinds.com/

Ware, B. (2019). *The Top Five Regrets of the Dying*. Amazon. Retrieved from https://bronnieware.com/blog/regrets-of-the-dying/

White, T. (2014, May 28). Retrieved from Stanford Medicine News Center: https://med.stanford.edu/news/all-news/2014/05/most-physicians-would-forgo-aggressive-treatment-for-themselves-.html

Wikipedia. (n.d.). *Doreen Lawrence*. Retrieved from https://en.wikipedia.org/wiki/Doreen_Lawrence

Woollacott, M. H. (2015). *Infinite Awareness*. Trio Alliance.

Worden, J. W. (2018). *Grief Counseling and Grief Therapy, Fifth Edition: A Handbook for the Mental Health Practitioner*. Springer Publishing Company.

Printed in Great Britain
by Amazon

42596508R00131